This book is available in quantity at special discounts for your group or organization.
For further information, contact:

Triumph Books LLC
814 North Franklin Street
Chicago, Illinois 60610
Phone: (312) 337-0747
www.triumphbooks.com

Printed in U.S.A.
ISBN: 978-1-63727-369-2

***DNVR* Nuggets Featured Writers & Hosts**
Adam Mares
Harrison Wind
Brendan Vogt
Eric Wedum
Duvalier Johnson
Mike Olson
Photographer: Ryan Greene

ALLCITY Network & *DNVR*
Adam Mares, VP of Content
Andre Simone, GM of *DNVR*
Alyssa Marye, *DNVR* Head of Production
Kalle Sorbo, *DNVR* Head of Live Streaming
Brandon Spano, ALLCITY Network CEO
Eric Wedum, ALLCITY VP of Creative
Ryan Koenigsberg, ALLCITY VP of Content
Allie Monroy, ALLCITY VP of Operations
Parker Sperry, ALLCITY Business Development

Content packaged by Mojo Media, Inc.
Joe Funk: Editor
Jason Hinman: Creative Director

Except where otherwise noted, all interior photos by Ryan Greene/*DNVR*

Front and back cover photos by Ryan Greene/*DNVR*

CONTENTS

INTRODUCTION

BY **ADAM MARES**

I remember the exact moment when the thought first crossed my mind that the Denver Nuggets were going to win an NBA championship. It was August 25, 2022 and I was sitting a few feet behind the baseline inside of Stark Arena in Belgrade, Serbia. On the far side of the court, Giannis Antetokounmpo had Nikola Jokic bottled up in the corner with the shot clock winding down and the game on the line.

We had traveled to Serbia to learn about the history and culture that delivered us the two-time MVP. We sampled the nation's cuisine, toured their city streets and got to know the people that make up a nation that has produced some of the most talented basketball players to ever play the game. It was the trip of a lifetime that culminated with the greatest basketball game any of us had ever watched.

The stakes for the game were high, with the winner earning a spot in the 2023 FIBA World Cup. It was also the first time in years that Jokic had played in front of a Serbian crowd and perhaps the only time in his life that he'd play a game of consequence in front of his countrymen.

Sitting courtside for the game were some of Serbia's greatest basketball legends of past, present, and future. There was Dejan Bodiroga, who won five gold medals for Serbia in international competition. There was Zeljko Obradovic, the most decorated coach in EuroLeague history. There was Novak Djokovic, the most decorated Tennis player of all time. Everybody who's anybody from Serbia was at the game with their eyes locked on Jokic, trapped in the corner with nowhere to go.

Jokic spun around to create the tiniest sliver of space and leaped off of his right foot to heave a Sombor Shuffle that miraculously found the bottom of the net.

An avid sports fan will go an entire lifetime without seeing such a moment of casual brilliance under immense pressure. I was certain that anyone who could make *that* shot in *that* moment was good enough to lead a team as star-crossed as the Denver Nuggets to an NBA championship.

The second time that I felt the Nuggets were going to win the championship was December 8, 2022. The Nuggets were on a three-game losing streak and Jamal Murray was 20 games into his return from a 500-day absence from the NBA following a torn ACL two seasons prior. Up until that point in the season, Murray looked like a shell of his former self. A step slower than before and lacking the swagger and confidence that defined his game before the injury.

But with six seconds in the game and the Nuggets trailing by two points, Murray danced with the basketball on the left wing before draining a game-winning shot over the out-stretched arms of his defender. If time had dulled the memory of the perfection under pressure that defined Murray before his injury, that shot reminded everyone just how extraordinary Murray always seemed to be when the game was on the line.

The Nuggets had spent several seasons piecing together a supporting cast that perfectly complemented their two stars. First, there was Michael Porter Jr, the 6-10 phenom with a perfect stroke who was the best prospect of his class until a

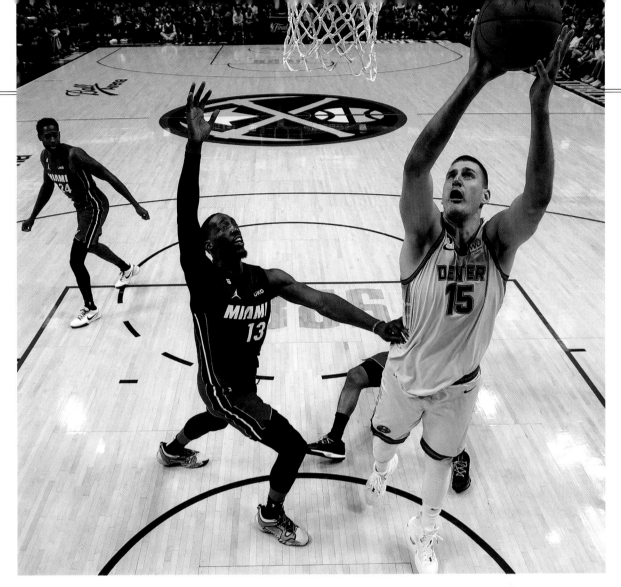

The journey to championship glory for Nikola Jokic and the Nuggets was a winding one that stretched from Serbia to Denver, but well worth every step along the way. (AP Images)

back injury threatened his career. The Nuggets took a chance on him in the belief that his upside was worth the risk that his injury presented.

There was Aaron Gordon, the defensive bully who could guard every position on the court but was miscast as a leading man with the Orlando Magic.

Lastly, there was Kentavious Caldwell-Pope, the two-way shooting guard who brought championship experience and veteran leadership.

Together, the group made a perfect basketball unit. Outstanding individuals who somehow combined to become greater than the sum of their parts. At their best, they could move in concert as if each play was choreographed and rehearsed for weeks before being performed.

For my entire life the thought of the Denver Nuggets winning a championship felt far-fetched and out of reach. 55 years had gone by since the franchise was founded, and 55 seasons had ended in heartbreak. Or worse, predictable disappointment. But on August 25, 2022, Nikola Jokic made the Sombor Shuffle, and suddenly anything felt possible.

10 months later, Jokic, Murray and the rest of the Denver Nuggets lifted the Larry O'Brien trophy to the cheers of 20,000 fans who had waited a lifetime for that very moment.

The golden era of Denver Nuggets basketball has finally arrived. 🖼

DNVR

NBA Finals, Game 1

JUNE 1, 2023
DENVER, COLORADO
NUGGETS 104, HEAT 93

OFF WITH A BANG

THE LIGHTS ARE NEVER TOO BRIGHT FOR NIKOLA JOKIC AND THE NUGGETS

BY **HARRISON WIND**

Ball Arena was buzzing. The stage was set. The lights were bright. There were feelings of tension but also anticipation spread throughout the building ahead of the first-ever NBA Finals game played in Denver.

As Nikola Jokic warmed up in the Nuggets' tunnel before taking the floor for layup lines, "In The Air Tonight" by Phil Collins blasted from the jumbotron. It felt like a landmark moment in Nuggets history, which this night absolutely was. Aaron Gordon took a moment during the National Anthem to soak it all in.

"I was like 'Wow, this is really the NBA Finals, and it's really, really cool,'" Gordon said.

But then Game 1 tipped off, and suddenly everything felt normal.

Jokic recorded another triple-double and finished with 27 points, 10 rebounds and 14 assists. Jamal Murray took over for portions of Game 1 and tallied 26 points, six rebounds and 10 assists in a game-high 44 minutes. Gordon used his physicality to bully Heat defenders inside and set the tone for the Nuggets with 12 of Denver's 29 first-quarter points while holding "Playoff" Jimmy Butler, who walked out of the Heat locker room postgame with a can of Michelob Ultra in hand, to his lowest-scoring game of the playoffs.

It felt like a typical Nuggets win, except taking Game 1 of the Finals is anything but typical.

There was a calmness to how the Nuggets operated while playing in the Finals spotlight for the first time. There was a poise to how Denver carried itself throughout all four quarters. The Nuggets played confident, relaxed and like the two-time MVP, looked ready and prepared for the moment even with the entire world's attention on them for the first time ever.

"To be honest, I couldn't wait to start, just because when the game started it felt normal," Nikola Jokic said after the Nuggets' 104-93 win, which wasn't as close as the score indicated. "Everything else didn't feel normal. The whole media day yesterday or the day before, I think people are making something bigger than it is. When the game started, I felt really comfortable."

How on earth is this dude so cool? Nothing can rattle Joker. Nothing can throw him off his game. His first Finals game was a walk in the park. It was really just another game to him. Watching Jokic operate, it felt like any other regular season matchup. Sometimes first-time Finals participants are rattled. Jokic patiently controlled the entire game.

He only attempted one shot in the first quarter and racked up six assists while letting Gordon eat the Heat's small-ball starting five alive in the paint. When Miami manufactured a brief late-game comeback,

Nikola Jokic powered the Nuggets to the first NBA Finals win in franchise history with 27 points, 10 rebounds and 14 assists.

Jokic then shifted into top gear and put in 12 fourth-quarter points to close the door on the Heat's run.

The Nuggets never panicked. They never lost their composure. They looked like a team that had been in the Finals and on this stage many times before.

"I think it's a standard that we hold ourselves to and that we have held ourselves to all year long," Gordon said about the Nuggets' poise. "We've been building habits day in and day out. So, you get to a game like this, the biggest stage in basketball, you let your standard of play and you let your habits carry you.

"We don't want to change too much. We want to go back to the film and look where we can get better. If we're looking to improve, I think we're in a good place."

The Nuggets look like they're ready to end this series before it's even started. Miami will adjust ahead of Game 2. Heat coach Erik Spoelstra is too good not to have a few tricks up his sleeve to slow Denver's attack and muster up a better offensive performance.

But good luck.

"Once we play the way we play," said Murray. "It doesn't really matter what the other team does."

The Nuggets are an offensive machine that can score in every way imaginable and hurt you from all angles. They proved that again in Game 1. Every member of their starting five is a threat. They can play any style and adapt to every type of fight. The Nuggets shot just 8-27 (29.6%) from 3-point range Thursday — their second-worst shooting performance of the playoffs — so Denver beat Miami with two's and held the Heat to just 93 points.

"This is just Denver Nugget basketball," Gordon said. "We find a mismatch, we exploit it and we keep going to it."

The Nuggets have only lost three games all playoffs. Two were Games 3 and 4 in Phoenix where Devin Booker shot a combined 34-43 for 83 points. The other was an OT loss in Minnesota. This team is a juggernaut. They have been all season and postseason long. They've dominated their competition in these playoffs by playing their way.

If this team keeps playing Denver Nuggets basketball, the Larry O'Brien trophy is coming to the Mile High City for the first time ever. ⌲

STAR SPOTLIGHT BY BRENDAN VOGT
NIKOLA JOKIC – A+

Nikola Jokic made history in his long-awaited Finals debut. Jokic joined Jason Kidd as the second player to record a triple-double in his first NBA Finals game. He's alone at the top with his 14 assists. And, of course, he did it all in a win. That's the only part that matters to him.

Jokic looked content as ever to stay true to his favorite basketball philosophy. A shot makes one person happy — an assist makes two. It's a lovely sentiment, although he might be wrong on the count. He made countless people from Chopper Circle, to York & Colfax, and the streets of Sombor elated by halftime. As the teams hit their locker rooms for a breather, Jokic had posted ten assists without turning the ball over once. He only shot three times. He didn't force it — "I never force it,"

he said after the game.

The Nuggets cruised through three quarters. They took center stage of the basketball universe and dazzled with their polished brand of basketball. They know how to win together. They understand why they've won together. They looked like a well-oiled, winning machine before the fourth quarter struck.

Miami junked it up with their coverages and leaned on their infamous zone defense. Haywood Highsmith (extremely cool name) began pressuring Jamal Murray full court. They forced Denver out of their beloved two-man game. The offense sputtered initially, and the Nuggets went to their first adjustment — let Jokic cook. The big fella carried them home with 12 points in the final quarter.

Aaron Gordon scored 12 of Denver's first 29 points on his way to 16 points and six rebounds.

JUNE 4, 2023
DENVER, COLORADO
HEAT 111, NUGGETS 108

DISCOMBOBULATED

FOR THE FIRST TIME ALL PLAYOFFS, THE NUGGETS DIDN'T LOOK LIKE THEMSELVES

BY **HARRISON WIND**

**We're talking about effort, and the Nuggets'
lack of it, in the NBA Finals.**

That's how a ticked-off Michael Malone opened his postgame press conference after the Nuggets' 111-108 Game 2 loss to the Miami Heat.

And he was right.

The Nuggets' lack of effort, but also their discipline, communication and overall focus wasn't at the level it needed to be. That's why Denver now finds itself in an NBA Finals matchup against the Heat that feels like it's just getting started.

"You guys probably thought I was just making up some storyline after Game 1 when I said we didn't play well. We didn't play well," said Malone. "Tonight, the starting lineup to start the game, it was 10-2 Miami. Start of the third quarter, they scored 11 points in two minutes and 10 seconds. We had guys out there that were just, whether feeling sorry for themselves for not making shots or thinking they can just turn it on or off, this is not the preseason, this is not the regular season. This is the NBA Finals. That to me is really, really perplexing, disappointing."

Jeff Green agreed with Malone's assessment.

"It's the fucking Finals, man," Denver's veteran said. "Our energy has to be better. We can't come out like we did, and we have to be better."

How the Nuggets lost Game 2 was shocking. Stunning. Surprising. It was a total out-of-character loss from a Denver team that's been locked in throughout the entire playoffs. The Heat shot 17-35

(48.6%) from 3-point range. So many of those attempts were wide open and came directly after defensive breakdowns and miscommunications that the Nuggets have avoided throughout most of this postseason.

"We weren't ourselves tonight," said Green.

The Nuggets weren't themselves — maybe for the first time all postseason — and it's because of their opponent. The Heat, an eight seed who nearly lost their second play-in game and missed the playoffs completely, are an entirely different team from the three Denver has faced so far on its run to the Finals.

Miami is incredibly tough. The Heat are disciplined, physical and aren't going to fold in the face of adversity. They're not going to make the same errors that the Suns or Lakers did. They're smart, well-coached and determined. They're going to capitalize on your miscues.

"They are punishing you as soon as you make mistakes," Nikola Jokic said. "Hopefully we're going to be disciplined for the next game."

They're not scared of the Nuggets either.

And in the first quarter of Game 2, the Nuggets looked a little scared. Miami ramped up its intensity and aggressiveness, and it felt like it got to Denver. The Nuggets looked rattled and soft, except for Jokic, whose 41 points, 11 rebounds and four assists weren't enough to carry his squad to victory. To open the first quarter, Denver was immediately back on its heels their heels. Some Nuggets players never regained their footing.

Nikola Jokic dropped 41 points and 11 rebounds on the Heat but had a tough time getting teammates involved in the Game 2 loss with only four assists.

Kentavious Caldwell-Pope, the only player on the Nuggets who's won a championship, didn't look like his typical steady self in Game 2. Caldwell-Pope fouled out in 36 minutes. Two of his fouls were on Heat 3-point attempts. Michael Porter Jr. shot 1-6 from 3-point range and is now shooting 3-17 through two Finals games. He looked discombobulated all night. I bet the Heat feel like they've gotten to Porter too.

That's why Game 3 will be so fascinating. The Heat have their confidence back. I guarantee you that they believe they're the tougher team. We're about to learn what the Nuggets are made of. How will every Nugget not-named Jokic bounce back on the road? Can Denver ramp its defensive intensity back up to where it's been for most of these playoffs?

"As I mentioned after Game 1, the fact that they got 16 wide-open threes was concerning. They didn't make them. So, we got lucky in Game 1," said Malone. "Tonight, they made them."

You could tell based on the Nuggets' postgame locker room that Denver took this loss hard. Porter and Caldwell-Pope exited before speaking with the media. Aaron Gordon was scheduled to go talk at the podium postgame but wasn't feeling well and also left the arena without speaking. Before he departed, Gordon sat at his locker for around 10 minutes straight with his head down and his hands over his face.

The Nuggets have a lot to think about before Game 3. Mainly, why did they suddenly rest on their laurels and forget what's gotten them to this point?

Moments after the Nuggets' first home defeat of the playoffs, Malone asked his team why they lost Sunday night.

Everyone knew the answer.

"Miami came in here and outworked us, and we were by far our least disciplined game of these 17 playoff games," Malone said.

We'll see how they respond. It's officially a series now. ⌲

NBA Finals, Game 3

JUNE 7, 2023
MIAMI, FLORIDA
NUGGETS 109, HEAT 94

DOUBLE DOSE OF DOMINATION

NIKOLA JOKIC AND JAMAL MURRAY ARE PROVING THEY'RE THE NBA'S TOP DUO

BY **HARRISON WIND**

Mike Miller was there from the beginning.

Before the title of "Best Player in the World" was his. Before the All-Star appearances, MVP's and before Nikola Jokic even earned a starting spot with the Nuggets, Miller was there to witness the earliest days of the golden era of Nuggets basketball. He joined the franchise prior to the start of the 2015-16 season, which was Jokic's rookie year. He saw the opening act of Jokic's Hall-of-Fame career first-hand.

Miller has always been a strong Jokic advocate, but did he ever see this happening? Did he see *this* level of greatness coming?

"I'm not going to sound like I'm crazy and say that I thought he'd be a two-time MVP and be on this stage like this. But I did, I really did," Miller told *DNVR* after the Nuggets' Game 3 win in Miami. "That's just how good he was and how good he is."

Jokic and Jamal Murray joined forces in Game 3 to lead the Nuggets to their biggest win in franchise history, a 109-94 triumph over the Heat to take a 2-1 series lead in the NBA Finals. The two-time MVP registered 32 points, 21 rebounds and 10 assists and became the first player in NBA Finals history to post a 30-20-10 game. Murray tallied a triple-double himself, finishing with 34 points, 10 rebounds and 10 assists. Jokic and Murray became the first pair of teammates in NBA history to record 30-point triple-doubles in the same game. Ever.

Murray hit dagger after dagger after dagger after dagger that staved off every Heat rally. He routinely drove by Jimmy Butler like he wasn't even there.

Miller, whose second season in Denver in 2016-17 coincided with Murray's rookie year, remembers his initial impression of the Blue Arrow too.

"Jamal has taken huge strides," Miller told *DNVR*. "He was always a guy that believed in himself. The moment was never too big, and he's showing that here."

Game 3 was a Jokic and Murray classic. It was a dominant, takeover performance from the Nuggets' two postseason stars who for now have assumed the title of Best Duo in the NBA. In Game 3, they picked apart a Miami defense that stymied Denver in Game 2. They busted the zone coverage that at times halted the

The Nuggets and Nikola Jokic got back in their groove in the Game 3 win as Jokic controlled the game with 32 points, 21 rebounds and 10 assists. (AP Images)

Nuggets' dynamic offense. They made the Heat's stout defense look ordinary.

Jokic and Murray combined for 64 of the Nuggets' 109 points. The Nuggets' third-leading scorer in Game 3 was rookie Christian Braun, whose 15 points gave Denver a needed boost off its bench. Jokic and Murray moved through the Heat defense all night with ease. Similar to how the Jokic-Murray two-man game closed the door on the Lakers in Game 3 of the Western Conference Finals, the Nuggets' duo was just too hot for the Heat to handle.

They danced together in the pick-and-roll. They ISO'd their defenders to death. They hurt Miami from the paint, mid-range, and beyond the arc. Their chemistry and synergy were on point. It was all on display for the world to see.

"I'd say it's a trust and a feel, that's the best way for me to put it," Murray said when describing his chemistry with Jokic. "It's not really X's and O's. It's just reading the game and trusting that the other is going to make the right play."

"If he throws it to me, he knows and expects what to see from me, and he knows the mood I'm in, the intensity I'm playing with, whether it's low or high, time and score, and vice versa. I know when he's overpassing, I know when he's looking to score, I know when he's the best player on the floor, I know when he's taking a second to get into the game."

It's a special sphere that Jokic and Murray are living in right now. That trust and feel isn't something that's learned overnight. It's been forged through years and years of on-court minutes together but also through the relationship and friendship that Jokic and Murray have built over the last seven seasons.

"A lot of guys play with each other. I think those two guys play for each other," said Malone.

You can't simply, create what they have overnight, throughout one regular season, or in one summer.

"The reality of the situation is they did it the right way in Denver," Miller told *DNVR*. "They did it through the draft, and they kept getting better."

After the Nuggets' Game 3 win, a content Denver locker room seemed satisfied with what they had just reminded the world of. These are the same Denver Nuggets that swept the Lakers and entered the NBA Finals with a 12-3 playoff record. This is the same juggernaut that breezed through most of the playoffs. Game 3 was a reminder to those in attendance at the Kaseya Center that the best duo in the NBA is a formidable, historical pairing that's on a mission.

Jokic sat at his locker after what right now can be considered the best game of his NBA career and re-fueled by taking down a container of watermelon piece by piece. On one side of his locker, a quote of his — curated by assistant coach Charles Klask and blown up on a poster by equipment manager Sparky Gonzalez — that was said after the Nuggets' clinched their first-ever trip to the NBA Finals tied a bow on a special night.

"We have a chance to do something nice."
– Nikola Jokic

Indeed they do.

"He hasn't changed much, to be honest," Miller told *DNVR* about Jokic. "The game's still slow for him. He still makes everyone around him better, and he goes and gets what he wants. He's just an impossible guard."

"He's a similar player to the guy he was back then. But now he's just in better shape now. He was always so skilled. Unbelievable size. Playmaking. Scorer. Touch has always been great. Just a great basketball player." ⌲

Jamal Murray joined Nikola Jokic on the triple-double train with 34 points, 10 rebounds and 10 assists — the first time in NBA Finals history that teammates had 30-point triple-doubles in the same game. (AP Images)

JUNE 9, 2023
MIAMI, FLORIDA
NUGGETS 108, HEAT 95

DIALED IN

WHAT IS NUGGETS CULTURE? THE HEAT FOUND OUT IN GAME 4

BY **HARRISON WIND**

We've heard a lot about "Heat Culture" throughout the Finals and in these playoffs.

"Hardest working," "most professional," and "best conditioned." Those were the words that flashed across the jumbotron in Miami prior to the start of Games 3 and 4 which describe the Heat's DNA.

But in Game 4 of the Finals, the Heat and the rest of the NBA learned about Nuggets Culture. They learned what Denver's team of destiny is all about. And they learned it while the back-to-back MVP and best player in the world was sitting on the bench in the fourth quarter.

"A big part of our culture is trusting one another," Michael Malone said after the Nuggets' 108-95 win that moved Denver to within one victory of its first NBA Championship.

That trust showed up late in Game 4. After Nikola Jokic was whistled for his fourth personal foul at the 9:41 mark of the fourth quarter and his fifth 27 seconds later, Malone turned to his bench. With Jokic sitting, a lineup featuring Jamal Murray, Kentavious Caldwell-Pope, Bruce Brown, Jeff Green and Aaron Gordon played the Heat nearly even and were only outscored by one point over the next five minutes of action.

It was a defining chapter in the story of this Nuggets team. Denver was run off the floor all regular season long with Jokic off the court but held its own without its superstar, on the road, in a raucous environment, during the highest-pressure minutes of the playoffs. Malone trusted that his group would get it done. They have for most of this postseason.

The Nuggets are +4 in the playoffs with Jokic off the court.

"Guys stepped up," said Malone. "We were up 13 going into the fourth quarter, they start off 8-0 and that coincides with Nikola picking up his fifth foul. So they came out aggressively. They have us on our heels, and usually in the regular season when Nikola went out, things kind of went haywire."

"But I can say not just tonight but throughout these playoffs, however many games we've played now, the non-Nikola minutes have gone really well. We called a timeout, we ran a play, ATO, Jamal knocks it down. Really well executed. The unit that was out there, Jamal, Bruce, Jeff, Aaron and then KCP or Christian, they defended."

The Nuggets somehow held their poise as Jokic trudged to the bench after a phantom fifth personal

Jamal Murray had a quiet night scoring with only 15 points but also added 12 assists in the big Game 4 win. (AP Images)

Nikola Jokic and the Nuggets took a commanding 3-1 series lead with the victory in Miami, leaving them just one win away from the first NBA title in franchise history. (AP Images)

foul was whistled by referee Scott Foster. Denver got enough stops, Green drilled a clutch corner 3, Gordon locked down on defense, and Brown took over.

Brown, one of the Nuggets' key offseason acquisitions who came to Denver to play defense, scored 11 of his 21 points in the fourth quarter. He hit the final dagger too, a pull-up 3 from the top of the arc with 1:21 remaining in regulation that clinched the Nuggets' win.

"When he did a step-back three, I almost — I wanted to punch him," Jokic said. "But when he made it, I was so happy."

If the Nuggets win Game 5 on Monday and bring the Larry O'Brien trophy to Denver for the first time in franchise history, that gutsy fourth-quarter spell from a lineup without Jokic will be remembered. It should be an iconic part of Nuggets history. There should be a place carved out at Ball Arena honoring that stretch of basketball.

Because no one would have batted an eye if

Denver had folded to Jimmy Butler, Bam Adebayo and Co. It would have been disappointing, sure, but there would have been a reason for it.

"All season long, it was like oh, the non-Nikola minutes," said Malone. "Kind of a crapshoot."

Not anymore.

The Nuggets can taste an NBA Championship. It's right there for the taking. Denver's mission is nearly complete. The Nuggets just took two games in Miami, a place where the Heat had only lost twice in the playoffs prior to Game 3 vs. Denver. They've had their foot heavy on the gas since they touched down in South Beach.

"I like that we didn't relax," Jokic said. "We didn't get comfortable. We were still desperate. We still want it. That's what makes me happy, that guys didn't relax."

With the ultimate goal now just 48 minutes away, owners Stan and Josh Kroenke sipped cans of Coors Light in the Nuggets' postgame locker room as they reminisced on a memorable win. Murray, the "Point God," as Gordon called him postgame following a 12-assist, zero-turnover night in a team-high 43 minutes, calmly sat at his locker that has a poster with a Bruce Lee quote taped to one side of it.

"Knowing is not enough. We must apply. Willing is not enough. We must do," it reads.

The Nuggets are on a path to accomplishing everything that they set out to do this season. They're on their way to fulfilling every goal that they had.

The elite defense that Denver said all along would be needed to win a championship has held the Heat under 100 points in three of four Finals games. Jokic is becoming an all-time great. Murray is proving that he's one of the best playoff performers in NBA history. Gordon is making it so the Nuggets' decision to acquire him back in 2021 is looked back on as the most momentous trade in franchise history. Malone is one win away from becoming the most outstanding coach to ever roam the Nuggets' sideline.

This is who the Nuggets always knew they could be.

"We believed and we knew how good we were for a few years now," Murray said. "So we're just focused, dialed in, and ready to do this thing."

"We're just ready to win a championship. We have the tools to do it. It's been on our minds for a while. We're just locked in. I don't think you've got to overthink it. We're just dialed in, ready to win." 🖼

STAR SPOTLIGHT BY BRENDAN VOGT
AARON GORDON – A+

Gordon isn't here for the credit. He's here for the wins. He doesn't have time for praise while so busy in the trenches. AG is a shapeshifter on defense, sizing up and down to assuage Denver's matchup concerns. He takes whatever form is needed to fill the cracks between the starters and raise the floor of the starting unit. Those are his duties. He only gets a few chances to shine on offense in a Nuggets uniform. But those years in Orlando were not a waste. Despite his penchant for the less glorified aspects of basketball, Gordon can put the ball through the hoop. He's no stranger to a big shot. He was unflinching in Game Four.

Gordon led all scorers with 27 points on a ridiculous 73% from the field. He shot 3-of-4 from deep, and the one miss was a desperate heave. The three makes were good before they left his hands. Mr. Nugget was locked in.

For most of the season, Michael Malone left AG as the backup five in his back pocket. Injuries forced his hand, and it's clear now Denver's head coach saw the obvious. It was the answer to the non-Jokic minutes. Once considered disastrous, they've survived that scenario multiple times on their path to a 3-1 lead in the Finals. That was the story Friday night, as a soft whistle gave Jokic his fifth personal foul. The others stepped up. None more so than Gordon.

NBA Finals, Game 5

JUNE 12, 2023
DENVER, COLORADO
NUGGETS 94, HEAT 89

WELCOME TO THE GOLDEN ERA

THE NUGGETS ARE FINALLY NBA CHAMPIONS

BY **HARRISON WIND**

Fresh out of college with a degree in mass communications from the University of Denver, Lisa Johnson sent in her resume and applied for a season ticket sales job with the Nuggets. Johnson had never worked in sales before but grew up watching the Nuggets and going to games. She simply wanted to work for her favorite team.

The Nuggets hired her on the spot, 42 years ago.

Johnson has been with the Nuggets ever since and is among the organization's longest-tenured employees. She eventually made the move from season ticket sales to basketball operations and began working as the receptionist for former head coach Doug Moe. In 1990, Johnson became the Nuggets' director of basketball administration. Eight years ago, Josh Kroenke and former Nuggets president of basketball operations Tim Connelly made her a Vice President.

Johnson has watched more Nuggets basketball than you and I combined.

Now, she's finally seen a championship.

"Winning a championship would be the greatest moment ever," she told *DNVR* around 24 hours before Game 5 of the NBA Finals between the Nuggets and Heat.

The Nuggets overcame a poor shooting game and an all-around ugly offensive night to eventually edge the Heat 94-89 to win their first NBA Championship in franchise history. Nikola Jokic finished with 28 points, 16 rebounds and four assists. Jamal Murray added 14 points, eight rebounds and eight assists. Michael Porter Jr. chipped in 16 points and 13 rebounds.

The Larry O'Brien trophy has a home in Denver. Finally.

It wasn't easy. It never was supposed to be. The first half of Game 5 was a slugfest. The Nuggets shot 1-15 from 3 and trailed the Heat 51-44 at the break. Bam Adebayo (18 points) outscored Jokic (nine points) and Murray (four points) combined.

But the Nuggets found their gear in the third quarter. Denver opened the second half on a 16-9 run. After struggling with his jumper throughout the Finals, Porter Jr. finally got a 3-pointer to fall late in the period. The Nuggets outscored the Heat 26-20 in the third and trailed by one heading to the fourth.

Nikola Jokic's daughter, Ognjena, was the center of attention as NBA commissioner Adam Silver presented the Larry O'Brien Trophy to the Nuggets.

In the end, it was Jokic who brought Denver home. The Finals MVP scored 10 points in the fourth quarter, and the Nuggets hit their free throws down the stretch to put the finishing touches on a dream season. The Nuggets went 16-4 on their way to their championship, which is tied for the second-best record by an NBA champion in a single postseason since 2003. It was a dominant run from a team that should be looked back on as a juggernaut.

This championship was made possible thanks to Jokic, Murray and the talented and versatile rotation that this front office has assembled over the last several years. The Nuggets' starting lineup fits like a glove. The roster just makes sense. Denver has the perfect combination of youth and veteran experience. The championship DNA of this team has been obvious since Day 1 of training camp. It all came together exactly like the Nuggets envisioned it would.

But this championship is not only for the players who celebrated in a champagne-soaked, cigar-smelling Nuggets locker room Monday night after Game 5. It's also for Johnson, who has given her heart and soul to this organization for 42 years. It's for people like Sparky Gonzalez, the Nuggets' equipment manager since 1987 who first befriended Jokic through pregame ping pong matches when he arrived in Denver as a rookie.

"Sparky is always in the background," Jokic said.

It's for people like Bobby Simmons, the Nuggets' director of security for the last two decades. It's for Vicki Ray, the Nuggets' loyal superfan who hasn't missed a home game in 32 years.

"I never thought the NBA would let this happen," Ray told *DNVR* after the Nuggets swept the Lakers.

It's for people like Ogi Stojakovic, the Nuggets assistant coach who predates Jokic's arrival in Denver

Michael Porter Jr. contributed 16 points and 13 rebounds to the championship-clinching win.

but has been the two-time MVP's trusted counsel over the last eight years. It's for people like Felipe Eichenberger, the Nuggets' head strength coach who was the first one who got Jokic to believe that he could be this great.

It's also for you, the loyal Mile High City diehards who became believers in an unorthodox second-round pick from Serbia and started to dream big.

That dream has become a reality.

The Nuggets are NBA Champions.

Above: Fans at Ball Arena were in a frenzy as Miami's Jimmy Butler stepped to the free throw line. Right: Jamal Murray speaks to the crowd during the celebration following the Nuggets' first NBA championship.

THE REST IS HISTORY

NIKOLA JOKIC ADDS TO HIS LEGEND AS NBA FINALS MVP

BY **HARRISON WIND**

Former Nuggets president of basketball operations Tim Connelly always liked to say that he got lucky when drafting Nikola Jokic in 2014.

And he's mostly right.

But what if it wasn't entirely luck? What if there was a little bit of instinct, a lot of intuition and a regrettable draft-day decision from 2007 that eat at Connelly for years and partly drove him to take a chance on Jokic in 2014?

In 2007, Connelly was working for the Washington Wizards, who held the 48th overall pick in the draft that year. When the draft shifted to the second round and the Wizards went on the clock at No. 48, an unorthodox center who had obvious talent but also came with countless question marks was still available.

The player in question had some obvious parallels to Jokic. He was an international big man who wasn't quick laterally and needed to get in better shape. He had a ton of talent but wasn't good defensively. He possessed world-class fundamentals and hands and projected as a quality shooter and scorer on the block. His basketball IQ was elite, and he just knew how to play the game. He wasn't a great athlete, but the potential was there.

The player was Marc Gasol.

The Wizards passed on Gasol and instead drafted Dominic McGuire, who at 6-foot-9 looked the part as an NBA small forward. He was definitely a safer pick than Gasol would have been. McGuire averaged 13.5 points and almost 10 rebounds per game at Fresno State and went on to play six NBA seasons. That's not bad for a second-round pick.

Gasol, of course, went on to win Defensive Player of the Year, make three All-Star teams, and was the starting center on the 2019 NBA Champion Toronto Raptors. With his international accomplishments, Gasol could eventually go into the Hall of Fame.

At No. 48 overall, one selection after Washington, Gasol was picked.

Connelly regretted not pounding the table harder for Gasol in the draft that year. Privately, he wished he had pushed harder to select him. So when Jokic, another unorthodox big man with obvious holes in his game but palpable potential, was available at 41st overall in 2014 and with the rest of Denver's front office on board, Connelly greenlit the selection.

The rest is history.

History was made Monday night at Ball Arena when the Nuggets clinched their first NBA Championship in franchise history with a 94-89 win

Nikola Jokic averaged 30.2 points, 14 rebounds and 7.2 assists in five games against Miami, earning Bill Russell NBA Finals Most Valuable Player honors.

over the Miami Heat in Game 5 of the NBA Finals. Jokic, the former second-round pick who was drafted during a Taco Bell commercial and over the last three years has ascended to the best basketball player in the world, was named the Bill Russell NBA Finals Most Valuable Player.

In Game 5, Jokic finished with 28 points (12-16 FG's), 16 rebounds and four assists. His 10 fourth-quarter points served as one final tour de force to end a season where Jokic played some of the most dominant basketball that the NBA has seen in years.

Jokic's Finals performance will go down as a convincing and undeniable run. His averages across five games against the Heat look like video game numbers: 30.2 points (58.3 FG%, 42.1 3P%), 14 rebounds and 7.2 assists per game.

Jokic tallied a 27-point, 10-rebound, 14-assist triple-double in Game 1. He went for 41 points in Game 2. In Game 3, Jokic recorded the first 30-point, 20-rebound, 10-assist game in NBA Finals history. Foul trouble kept Jokic to a 23-12-4 line in Game 4, but in a closeout Game 5, Jokic was the only one who Denver could count on for consistent offense. He scored 19 of his game-high 28 points in the second half.

This postseason, Jokic became the first player in NBA history to lead the playoffs in total points, rebounds and assists.

"I seen a picture of Jok and Embiid running for MVP, and Jok keeps running," Jamal Murray said after the Nuggets clinched the championship. "I think that just speaks so much to what his mindset is. I got mad at him today in the game because he kept passing the ball. I hit him in the pocket, he has a floater and he'd pass it. Out of bound, turnover. I'm like, bro, just shoot it."

"Jok is the Finals MVP and rightfully so and deserving, and he makes everybody connect and everybody want to win being so unselfish."

With a championship and a Finals MVP to his name, Jokic is automatically an all-time great. Now, we find out how high he can climb. He's unlike anything we've ever witnessed or probably will witness again in the NBA. He's arguably the greatest passer in league history. He's a force of nature on the offensive end of the floor and one of the most dominant individual hubs of offense that the NBA has ever seen. He outsmarts his competition every night. He's completely selfless and just wants to win. And that's what he made sure happened Monday in Game 5.

Denver is lucky to have him. And Connelly was somewhat lucky to draft him.

"We are not winning for ourselves," Jokic said after he was handed the Finals MVP. "We are winning for the guy next to us."

Jokic is the Denver Nuggets. He's the face of this city and this franchise. He's the central reason why the Nuggets captured their first NBA Championship.

And he's why Denver could rack up a few more Larry O'Brien trophies over the next several years. 🖼

In the 2023 postseason, Nikola Jokic became the first player to lead the playoffs in total points, rebounds and assists. (AP Images)

ROAD TO THE TITLE

CHAMPIONSHIP VISION

INSIDE CALVIN BOOTH'S PLANS TO BRING A CHAMPIONSHIP TO DENVER

BY **HARRISON WIND** · JULY 13, 2022

Calvin Booth's front office career was born during the 2008-09 season while he was still wearing a Sacramento Kings jersey.

It was the final season of his 10-year playing career and Booth would only appear in eight games. Naturally, as the season wore on and his minutes decreased, Booth thought about what was next and the possibility of one day working in a front office.

So from the end of the Kings' bench, Booth began to pay increased attention to the art of team building. Why were teams and rosters built in the way they were? What types of skill-sets and personalities mixed best on the floor? How were different franchises able to effectively surround their star with the right kind of role players?

"I had a front row seat to watch the best players in the world, learn how teams were constructed, and what worked and didn't work," Booth told *DNVR*. "It was the best education I could have asked for."

It was during those final months of his NBA career when Booth first began to develop his vision for how to construct an NBA-championship roster.

Finishing the job

After starting his front office career as a scout with the Pelicans, Booth took a job with the Timberwolves a year later and worked his way up to Minnesota's director of player personnel. Tim Connelly, who was the assistant GM in New Orleans when Booth worked there, then hired him in Denver in 2017 to be his assistant GM and No. 2 executive.

As Denver grew into a championship contender, Booth grew into a highly-respected executive around the league. He interviewed for the Timberwolves general manager opening in 2019 and the Kings GM job in 2020. But Connelly's sudden departure to Minnesota earlier this offseason placed Booth in a position he never expected to be in. Booth always figured that if he did get the opportunity to run a team, that it would be a rebuild, not a contender on the doorstep or an NBA championship.

"I never thought I'd be, you know, the steward of a team of this caliber in my very first job," he said.

There's a quiet confidence that Booth has carried with him into this role. It mainly comes from the

Rookie Christian Braun fits general manager Calvin Booth's vision of a big guard who can defend but also has high upside as a scorer.

fact that he was here to help lay the foundation of this roster with Connelly. He has worked alongside Michael Malone since fairly early on in the Nikola Jokic era. He has watched up close as Jamal Murray grew into an All-Star level player. He has tracked Jokic's development from starter to All-NBA talent to back-to-back MVP. He has thoroughly analyzed what types of role players around Jokic and Denver's big 3 work and which ones don't.

"The hard part about where I'm at right now is we've done a great job. Tim and Coach Malone and Mr. K and Josh, all of our best players getting us to this point, and now you're inside the 10-yard line and the job becomes really, really hard," Booth said. "But on the other side, what's really easy is I know what Coach Malone likes. I have a feeling or a vision for the kind of guys, Nikola, Jamal or Michael would like to play with, and it just happens to be in line with my philosophy anyway."

Based on what he's done in his first offseason running the Nuggets, Booth's vision appears crystal clear. He entered the summer wanting to add more defensive-minded players with size to the Nuggets' roster. He did that in his first move this summer by trading for Kentavious Caldwell-Pope in exchange for Will Barton and Monte Morris. Denver also got reserve point guard Ish Smith in the deal, but Caldwell-Pope was the main prize.

In the lead-up to this offseason, the Nuggets surveyed the league for available two-guards. They came away believing the 6-foot-5 Caldwell-Pope was the best available player and fit based on guards that Denver deemed gettable. Of course, there was competition for his services. In conversations prior to the trade, Caldwell-Pope's agent Rich Paul told Booth that the Wizards' shooting guard was in high demand around the league. Booth knew he had to act swiftly to nab him before someone else did. Many teams wanted Caldwell-Pope's championship pedigree and high-level role player skill-set.

Bruce Brown also fit Booth's vision for how to surround Jokic and Denver's offensive talent. He's a big guard at 6-foot-4 with a 6-9 wingspan who's a high-level defender. Booth believes he can play point guard, shooting guard and small forward in some lineups. I'd look for the Nuggets to use Brown similarly to how Denver deployed PJ Dozier last season as a versatile ball handler who can play with a multitude of lineups and players.

"He was right at the top of our list," Booth told *DNVR* of Brown. "He was the guy for us."

Brown was coveted around the NBA, but Denver was able to nab him for the taxpayer mid-level exception. I asked Brown in Las Vegas this week if he turned down more money to sign with the Nuggets and play with Jokic. He didn't come out and say he did, but Brown didn't give the greatest poker face either.

Booth's other free agent addition, DeAndre Jordan, led to some backlash. Jordan bounced between the Lakers and 76ers last season and appeared in 48 games. By December he was out of the Lakers' rotation. After signing with the 76ers in March, he stuck with Philadelphia's bench unit during the regular season but lost his rotation spot to second-year backup big Paul Reed in the playoffs.

From what I can tell, here was Denver's thinking in bringing in Jordan: The Nuggets thoroughly surveyed the market — let's not pretend that these deals and signings aren't decided before free agency begins — and liked some of the intangibles that Jordan brought to the table. Jordan is a culture guy and well-liked throughout NBA locker rooms, which was a big selling point for Denver. I don't know how many other true backup centers were willing to come to Denver

Veteran Jeff Green has been a perfect fit as a versatile big man off the bench for two seasons with the Nuggets.

and play a small role behind Jokic on a minimum contract either. Maybe most importantly, he's a rim roller. That's something Denver wanted to prioritize in a backup center. I think the Nuggets will also aim to play Jeff Green at backup center, which is his best position, throughout the season too.

Those three moves, but the Caldwell-Pope and Brown acquisitions in particular, shaped Booth's first offseason at the Nuggets' helm.

Drafting the future

Booth was never a star throughout his playing career. The self-described journeyman filled a lot of different roles as he bounced between seven teams during his 12 years in the NBA.

He was drafted 35th overall by the Wizards in 1999. Two years later, Booth signed a six-year contract with Seattle and started 40 of 133 games over the next three seasons. His career-high 24-points came in a 2001 win over Dallas where Booth shot a perfect 12-12 from the free-throw line. In 2004, Booth recorded a career-high 10 blocks in only 17 minutes against the Cavaliers and a 19-year-old rookie named LeBron James.

His shining moment as a pro came in Game 5 of the 2001 playoffs. Booth made the game-winning layup with 9.8 seconds remaining to give the Dallas Mavericks a 3-2 series lead over Utah Jazz. It would be the Mavs' first playoff series win since 1988.

Booth's varied background as a role player has given him a unique perspective on scouting and roster building. He has seen what works and what doesn't in this league. He has watched role players come and go. He has seen highly-regarded prospects bust and unheralded, under-the-radar draft picks go on to have storied careers. He knows the work ethic, attitude and day-in-day-out approach that's needed to make it in this league.

Booth is highly, highly respected within the Nuggets and around the NBA as a scout. Prior to Connelly leaving Denver, Booth was already leading weekly Zoom calls with the Nuggets' front office where staffers discussed and debated players and prospects. He has been running the Nuggets' day-to-day for at least the last year.

"He's the best talent evaluator I have ever been around," one high-ranking NBA scout told *DNVR*.

In Booth's two first-round draft picks this summer, you saw his roster-building philosophy on full display. In Christian Braun, Booth nabbed someone in the draft who he believes has an incredibly high floor but can also develop into an upper-level role player. At 6-foot-7, Braun fits Booth's vision as both a bigger guard and one who's defensive-minded. I don't think you'll see the Nuggets under Booth's guidance bring in a smaller guard who doesn't defend. It just doesn't fit his vision.

Braun's skill-set and intangibles will eventually complement Jokic and Denver's high-volume scorers, maybe as soon as this coming season. Booth believes that Braun's motor, competitive spirit and fearlessness will lead him to having a long NBA career. The Nuggets inquired about trading up into the lottery on draft night, but a deal never came to fruition. In the end, they were more than OK betting on Braun.

Booth is as thorough as they come in the lead-up to the draft, and he used all the information at his disposal to select Peyton Watson 30th overall. Watson barely played as a freshman at UCLA after joining a loaded roster that returned all five starters and 10 players total from last year's Final 4 team. But the five-star recruit did have moments throughout the season where he flashed upside, particularly on the defensive end of the floor. Booth was also in attendance when Watson scored a season-high 19 points on 9-12 shooting in an early-season win over Bellarmine.

While Peyton Watson played sporadically as a rookie, he flashed enough potential to be a good match for Calvin Booth's long-term outlook for the team.

The Nuggets' front office did their due diligence on Watson's background too. Booth came away impressed with his passion for the game and drive. It was an all-encompassing scouting process where Denver had to look at the full picture when it came to the 6-foot-8 small forward with a 7-1 wingspan.

"I think you need all aspects of information when evaluating players, but I think sometimes people overlook certain things," Booth told *DNVR*. "If I was only data-driven on the Peyton Watson decision, I don't know if I would have taken him. But my experience as an NBA player and seeing guys like that and seeing how other players respond to that guy on the floor is all part of our discourse in the room."

Learning the role, and the MVP

Booth arrived back in Denver at the start of free agency after a quick trip to Sombor, Serbia. There he broke bread with the back-to-back MVP who's enjoying his offseason back home alongside his family and friends.

The two kept their conversation light. Over dinner, Booth discussed his plans for the roster with Jokic, but they also spoke about life and topics outside of basketball. The offseason gives Jokic time to disconnect from the NBA world and be surrounded by his close circle, his family and his horses during the summer months. It's something that Booth, who's a family man himself, and the Nuggets respect and honor.

"One thing I can appreciate about Nikola is his ability to be present and enjoy where he's at," Booth said. "That's a special skill to be able to have. He can rest, recuperate, recharge and then get ready to make another run at it."

It was Booth's first time to Sombor and the check-in with Jokic is a responsibility that now falls on his shoulders as the Nuggets' top basketball executive.

It's one that he's more than happy to take on. Booth loves talking shop with anyone, whether that's the best basketball player on the planet or the last guy on his roster. That's just who he is.

Booth will sit for hours, like he did over the last week in Las Vegas, and just watch basketball. He's addicted to the sport. It doesn't matter the level of the prospect he's watching or the magnitude of the game, Booth is always jonesing for more hoop. Any level, any venue, any stage, Booth's burning desire to learn more about a player or the game never stops.

That passion and humility helped Booth get to this point in his career. His dedication to his craft and the respect he's garnered from his peers led to Josh Kroenke entrusting him after Connelly left the organization in May.

"You have to be at the right place at the right time to get a job like this, obviously," Booth told *DNVR*. "Being in this position, I'm lucky. We all make mistakes from time to time, but you always try to correct them on the fly and go back and see why they were made so you don't make them again."

It's an opportunity that Booth doesn't take lightly. Booth feels a responsibility to steer the Nuggets towards a championship and maximize Jokic's prime. He knows the expectations that are riding on this season. It's why he entered the summer with such an aggressive mindset.

He saw an opportunity to improve this roster with his vision and took it.

"We have a two-time MVP," Booth said. "And we feel like we've surrounded him with the pieces that should put us in position to win a championship next season." ⊡

Acquired in an offseason trade with the Wizards, the addition of dynamic guard Kentavious Caldwell-Pope may have been one of the most notable moves in the league leading up to the 2022-2023 NBA season.

TIME TO BELIEVE

NEW SEASON BRINGS RENEWED HOPE TO DENVER

BY **HARRISON WIND** · OCTOBER 3, 2022

Do you remember what it felt like when the Nuggets traded for Aaron Gordon in March of 2021?

March 28: Nuggets beat the Hawks 126-102 in Gordon's debut

Gordon finished with 13 points on 6-9 shooting. Nikola Jokic, Jamal Murray and Michael Porter Jr. combined for 48 points on 20-35 (57%) shooting.

"I see no limits for this team," Gordon said postgame that night. "It looks like we have all the pieces for this team, we have depth. We're covered in a lot of different spots. As long as we're working together there's no stopping us."

March 30: Nuggets beat the 76ers 104-95

Playing in front of fans for the first time since the pandemic started, Denver outscored Philadelphia 44-24 in the first quarter and coasted to a win.

Michael Porter Jr. was turning into Klay Thompson and only used only four dribbles to score 27 points.

April 1: Nuggets beat the Clippers 101-94

The Nuggets handed out 28 assists on their 39 made baskets to beat the Clippers and Kawhi Leonard.

Michael Malone said his players seemed rejuvenated and he sensed a "renewed excitement" after the Gordon trade. "You can feel it in the locker room."

"We feel like we're complete," said Will Barton. "We feel like this is the team. We feel like we have enough to go all the way…(a championship) is definitely our goal. We can't shy away from it. We can't run from it."

April 1: Nuggets beat the Clippers 101-94

Denver came out lax but outscored Orlando 72-44 in the second half to get its fourth-straight win. Gordon had 24 points on 10-13 shooting and seven rebounds. Jokic had 17 points, nine rebounds and 16 assists. Porter Jr. added 20 points on and 12 rebounds on 8-14 shooting. Murray had 22 points, five rebounds and three assists.

"It's a testament to where this team can go," Gordon said that night regarding the comeback.

The Nuggets went on to win their first seven games following the Gordon trade. With Jokic, Murray, Porter Jr. and Gordon on the floor, Denver outscored its opponent by 46 points in 117 minutes. That quartet produced a 126.4 Offensive Rating, a 108.2 Defensive Rating and an 18.2 Net Rating when on the court together. They scored, defended, rebounded, assisted

and played basketball at a ridiculously high level. Then…Denver then lost at home vs. the Celtics on April 11th and then again at the Warriors one night later when Jamal Murray tore his ACL.

But if you remember the two weeks after that Gordon trade right up until the waning moments that night in Golden State, you remember the feeling you had while watching this team. You remember the excitement following the all-in trade deadline move made by the Nuggets' front office. You remember the ease at which the Nuggets' offense flowed. You remember how it felt like Denver could get a layup or open three every single trip down the floor. You remember the efficiency, the versatility, the two-way play that Denver packed. You remember thinking that the Nuggets finally had all the pieces.

You remember thinking about a championship.

For the first time in 18 months, you can think those same thoughts again. Murray is back. So is Porter Jr. With Kentavious Caldwell-Pope, the Nuggets have arguably the best starting five in the league. Gordon, Caldwell-Pope and Bruce Brown give Denver more top-tier defensive options than the Nuggets have had in recent memory. This is by far the most complete team that I've seen in Denver in the Jokic era.

Tonight is just preseason game No. 1. Denver still has a long way to go just to begin to achieve the lofty goals that this group has set for itself. But tonight is when the foundation for this season begins to get laid. This is when the Jokic-Murray-Porter trio first begin to re-establishes the chemistry that they were quickly building in 2021. This is when Gordon, Caldwell-Pope, Brown, Bones Hyland and Denver's role players start to mesh. This is when Malone begins to learn what this group actually looks like on the floor. It's the first time in 18 months that Jokic, Murray, Porter Jr. and Gordon could all be on the floor together.

At training camp in San Diego, those same feelings that we all felt post-trade deadline in 2021 resurfaced. There's this quiet confidence around the Nuggets right now that has you thinking big. The Nuggets are walking with a strut and a swagger. There's a level of maturity to this team right now that I've never seen before. There's a sense of poise and readiness for the task that awaits.

"It's a different vibe," Gordon said last week. "I think we've got some of our guys back. We got [Murray] back. I think that's kind of what picks the vibe up. Level of excitement, we're always excited. I'm always excited. We're always excited. But for me, there's a certain level of calmness, just because we have so many great guys on this team. We have such a talented roster. You can lean on your brothers on this team. That is bringing me a certain level of peace."

This Nuggets team has everything needed to win a championship. It has the star power in Jokic. It has the supporting cast in Murray, Porter Jr. and Gordon. It has the championship-caliber role players in Caldwell-Pope and Brown that every contender needs. It has the veterans in Jeff Green and DeAndre Jordan to tie this group together. It has an experienced head coach who's been through his fair share of playoff battles.

As was the case after the 2021 trade deadline, it's officially time to start believing in the Nuggets again. 🖾

Finally fully healthy, the starting five of the Nuggets is as talented as any in the NBA.

27

POINT GUARD

JAMAL MURRAY

INSIDE STAR GUARD'S MUCH ANTICIPATED RETURN

BY **HARRISON WIND** · OCTOBER 4, 2022

539 days away from the game, nearly 18 months, a tiring rehab and an endless amount of reps on the practice court. All for this moment.

Jamal Murray returned Monday night at Ball Arena. It was just Denver's preseason opener and played in front of only around 12,000 people, but it was a moment that Murray, the Nuggets' organization, and its fans have been waiting for, for what seemed like forever.

Here's how the night unfolded.

6:00 pm: Murray takes the floor for warmups

Murray went through the typical pre-game warmup that he did every game before his injury. It starts with form shooting from the restricted area and expands to mid-range jumpers, both off the catch and off the dribble. Murray then goes around the 3-point arc, making shots at seven different spots. Next is 1-on-1 work with Denver's player development coaches. Murray starts at around half-court, dribbles at his defender and works on his pull-up jumper, both from 3 and mid-range.

Since the injury, Murray hasn't altered his pregame routine too much. He still gets to the arena around the same time every day and goes through the same warmup. The only change he's added is an extra 10 minutes for stretching.

Prior to his warmup tonight, Murray chatted with his father, Roger, who flew in for the game and will be in town for a bit.

7:10 pm: Pregame introductions

Nikola Jokic always gets introduced first during pregame player intros. It's been the case since a few games into the 2018-19 season when he switched from being introduced last to first. Ever since the switch, Murray (when he's played) gets introduced last.

It was a really cool moment finally hearing Murray's name called again by Nuggets public address announcer Kyle Speller. It felt like a return to Nuggets normalcy. It felt right.

After he was introduced, Murray got mobbed by his teammates.

1st quarter, 7:09 remaining: Murray misses his first free-throw

Murray missed his first shot of the game. He clanged

Jamal Murray's absence from the court was an extended one, but his patience paid off to great results as he grew increasingly more comfortable throughout the season.

step-back deep two early in the first quarter. Then after a Thunder technical, Murray walked to the free-throw line with his first point of the night there for the taking.

The 88% career free-throw shooter couldn't keep it together. He missed.

"I was laughing," Murray. "Joker said, 'Go shoot it.' I was walking by, 'OK, I'm about to make my shot right here,' and everybody started cheering. I was like, 'Ah damn!' And I started smiling. It got to my head."

Murray missed his next shot too. Out of a timeout and off a designed play-call, he drew iron on a 3-pointer from the top of the arc.

"I felt like a rookie out there," he said. "The faster pace. On a couple closeouts, I was like, 'Man, he was coming on pretty fast,' but he really wasn't, so I rushed a couple shots I could make. The game was moving a lot faster than I expected. Then on top of that, the adrenaline. Then, on top of that, I missed my first couple. I was like, 'Damn, I missed a free throw.'"

2nd quarter, 6:19 remaining: Murray's first basket

Murray got on the board shortly after he checked back for his second stint of the game during the second quarter. Ish Smith found him in the corner on a Nuggets fastbreak. Swish.

"Obviously, there was a lot of excitement," said Murray. "It's been a while. Like I said, I don't really care if I don't score, I did care a little bit."

"When I sat down, ultimately the nerves settled. I got relaxed and I just went out there and played. It was good, it was a good feeling. I had a lot of fun and like I said, I'm just happy to be out there."

2nd quarter, 1:27 remaining: The Murray-Jokic pick-and-roll leads to a Michael Porter Jr. 3

Murray's corner 3 got him in a rhythm. He then powered through Tre Mann in the post for a tough

layup. After that, Murray stuck a step-back 3 right in Josh Giddey's eye. He also started to get into the two-man game with his favorite pick-and-roll partner. Murray and Jokic fell into that familiar action several times Monday night.

This one led to a Porter Jr. 3.

"I was very excited for him," Porter Jr. said. "I was almost happier for him than I was for myself. Seeing him hit that big shot and the crowd go crazy, he makes the game so much easier for all of us. He's a big piece if we ever want to be a championship team. He's a very, very big part of that. I was just happy to see him out there and smiling, even when he didn't make the first couple of shots. Just to see that he was fine. He's a team player and he's there to win."

2nd quarter buzzer: A signature shot

Murray loves to take and make big shots. He loves the pressure, the moment, the eyeballs, and everything that comes with those situations. He got one of those moments at the end of the second quarter.

Murray dribbled the length of the floor with 6.6 seconds remaining in the half and eventually got a step on Kenrich Williams while going to his left. He jumped off his left foot while drifting left and sunk this leaner high off the glass.

The pent-up emotion from the last 539 days spilled out.

"That's what I do!" Murray shouted after the buzzer-beater.

"That's what I do. That's exactly what I said," Murray admitted postgame. "I haven't been in that mode in a while, you know. I haven't been locked in for what it feels like is the last couple of years. Just to be locked in, I had that mentally from a few years ago. Just to bring that out at the start of the year, I was just excited."

That shot was the capper on a successful debut, even though the Nuggets lost their preseason opener 112-101. Murray was expectedly rusty in the first quarter but settled in quickly. He even flashed for a couple of possessions. Those moments felt like the old Jamal Murray.

Murray's final line: 10 points (4-7 FGs, 2-3 3 FGs), two rebounds, two assists and two turnovers in 15 minutes. After halftime, he and Denver's starters' nights were over.

Now comes rest and recovery — something he hasn't done yet after a game — before Denver's second preseason matchup Friday in Chicago. Murray said late Monday night that he felt good immediately following the game.

"It's a checkmark for sure," Murray said. "It's one of those mental checks just to be out there and feel it and move on from there. Got my feel. Felt the crowd. Felt the team, the ball moment, moving on the floor. Just all of that. It's different than practice. It's way different. It was just a lot of fun."

Monday night was a big step. It was a checkmark, as Murray put it. He can cross it off the list. He finally played in a game again.

There's still a long road ahead, but at least for Murray that road now has a map. He'll gradually become more comfortable on the floor. He'll build up his game little by little. He'll work to mesh with Jokic, Porter and his teammates. His minutes will increase as he rediscovers his game.

It all won't come back at once. Slowly but surely he'll become Jamal Murray again. Those signature moments, like the one he had Monday, will become more frequent. The step-back 3s will continue to go in at higher and higher rates. His floor game will become smoother by the minute. But the hard part is out of the way.

"This is gonna be a hell of a year," Murray said. 📷

Jamal Murray's prediction that "this is gonna be a hell of a year" was more prophetic than he could've realized.

SMALL FORWARD

BRUCE BROWN

MEET THE MOST UNIQUE PLAYER IN THE NBA

BY **HARRISON WIND** · OCTOBER 13, 2022

Bruce Brown, the golfer, was born in 2020.
The pandemic hit, the NBA suspended the season, and Brown decided to hit the driving range with some friends. The next day he bought a set of clubs. 24 hours later he was on a course. Brown was hooked.

When he's back home in Boston during the summer, Brown plays golf 2-3 times per week. He's a member of TPC Boston, a private club in Norton, Massachusetts. Brown's handicap is 14 after only playing for two years. He eventually wants to get it down to a 1 or a 2.

Golf is one of the reasons why Brown already loves life as a Denver Nugget. The thin Mile High air carries the golf ball just a little bit further. In Colorado, Brown's driving 320 yards with regularity.

"I hit bombs here," Brown told *DNVR* at training camp earlier this month. "I hit absolute bombs."

Brown is maybe the most unique player in the NBA, on and off the court. Not a lot of NBA players have a handicap in the low teens. Not a lot of NBA players love country music either. Brown's a country boy at heart. Luke Combs, Morgan Wallen, Dan + Shay, Dustin Lynch and Jordan Davis are featured

heavily in his Spotify rotation. Combs' tour doesn't stop in Denver this year, much to Brown's chagrin, but he's already planning to rock out at his concert in Massachusetts next summer.

"I don't think anyone on this team is into country. Luke Kennard, my teammate in Detroit, was into it, but that's about it," Brown said. "Definitely no one in New York."

He's also one-of-a-kind between the lines. Brown came into the league as a 6-4 point guard and bulldog defender for the Pistons, but over the last two seasons in Brooklyn, Brown played as more of a "rover" instead of an actual position. With the Nets, he shuffled between shooting guard, small forward, power forward and center in an offense designed to get Kevin Durant and Kyrie Irving shots.

In pick-and-rolls last season, Brown logged more total possessions than Aaron Gordon as the roll man and fewer possessions than Bryn Forbes as the ball-handler. He registered just one fewer screen assist than Pascal Siakam and Jaren Jackson Jr. In Brooklyn, only 15% of Brown's shots came from 3-point range, which placed him in the bottom-5 percentile among all

Bruce Brown's unique combination of defensive versatility and timely offensive contributions were the ideal addition to Denver's roster.

forwards, and 68% of his field goal attempts came in the paint. He was a guard masquerading as a 7-footer.

Brown was asked this preseason if he would rather be the ball handler or screener in the pick-and-roll with Nikola Jokic. His answer wasn't typical of a 6-foot-4 guard.

"Me screening for Joker," he said. "Easy."

With the Nets, Brown guarded every position on the floor and earned the reputation as one of the most dependable defenders in the league. Brown has a rock-solid frame, quick feet, and packs a 6-9 wingspan. He rarely gets hurt. He lives to defend and wants the toughest defensive assignments every night.

Offense never came easy to Brown. He remembers routinely blowing easy layups when he was younger. It just was never his thing, so he naturally gravitated toward defense. If the Nuggets want to achieve their lofty goal of finishing the season as a top-5 defense, Brown will have to be front-and-center all year.

When he was available in free agency this summer, Michael Malone phoned general manager Calvin Booth.

"Hey man, this is a guy that we need," Malone said.

Brown had options, but picking Denver and signing a two-year, $13.3 million deal was an easy choice he says. He looked at it as the perfect setting for the next chapter of his career. He can contend for a championship and be relied upon defensively to set the tone. That's what Brown wants. He wants that responsibility. He wants the pressure of guarding All-NBA offensive players. He wants that burden resting on his shoulders.

"I know why I'm here," Brown said. "I'm here to play defense."

In the Nuggets' preseason win over the Suns, Brown guarded Devin Booker and held the Suns' guard to 20 points on 5-17 shooting. It earned him the Nuggets' first Defensive Player of the Game chain of the season.

"I knew Devin Booker was going to come out and be really aggressive," Brown said while wearing a baby blue hat emblazoned with a yellow and green Masters golf tournament logo. "I played him for the last five years, so I knew what I was getting myself into tonight."

Brown plays with a level of effort, energy and tenacity that we haven't seen in Denver in a long time. He covers so much ground on defense in such a little amount of time. He has incredible closeout speed. He's a multiple-effort player who gets out and contests shots on the perimeter that he has no business contesting. Brown floats into passing lanes on just feel and instincts.

He was one of only five players (Matisse Thybulle, De'Anthony Melton, Gary Payton II, Killian Hayes) to record at least 160 deflections in 1800 or fewer minutes last year. Brown gets skinny, stays with his matchup, and slips around the same screens that so many recent Nuggets defenders routinely died on over the last several seasons. Brown's defensive IQ is through the roof.

He's the exact type of defender that the Nuggets have desperately needed for years.

"That guy is a pro. He's a five-year pro who carries himself like a 10-year pro. He knows exactly who he is as a player," Malone said. "He doesn't work on things that are not in his wheelhouse. I have a feeling that Bruce Brown will close a lot of big games for us."

The Nuggets signed Bruce Brown away from the Nets in what turned out to be a bargain deal at two-years for $13.3 million.

Brown is now on the right side of the matchup that gave him so many headaches over the last couple of years. Playing in the Eastern Conference for his entire four-year career, Brown only faced off against the Nuggets twice per season. He's had some standout games versus Denver too. Brown went for 19 points on 7-10 shooting, 10 rebounds and eight assists in a 2020 Nets win over the Nuggets. He tallied 16 points on 8-11 shooting, six rebounds, three assists and three blocks in a 2021 Brooklyn victory.

But he always hated trying to craft a defensive scheme to stop the back-to-back MVP. He hated playing against the Nuggets.

"Nikola was a fucking beast to play against," said Brown. "Every time I played against him it seemed like he had 40."

Now, the two have joined forces. One of Brown's principal qualities is his ability to fit with any lineup and alongside any group of players. He can play on and off the ball. He started at point guard Wednesday vs. the Clippers and don't be surprised when Brown is handling the ball at times alongside Bones Hyland on the Nuggets' second unit. Denver wants to move him back to more of his natural position on the perimeter. It's a transition Brown has said he's more than OK with.

Brown is a masterful cutter and off-ball mover too. The prospect of him playing alongside Jokic, Jamal Murray and Michael Porter Jr. is enticing because of Brown's ability to find creases in the defense that few others can. It's a skill set that was built up partly due to Brown's sky-high on-court awareness, but also after playing alongside high-caliber offensive talent the last couple of seasons. He finds a way to make stuff happen without having any plays called for him.

The University of Miami product comes to Denver with big-game experience and 20 career playoff games under his belt. Last postseason, his first-round assignment was Jayson Tatum in a series and matchup that Malone has studied closely since Denver inked Brown to a contract. Brown already has the trust of his coach and teammates, especially the ones he's gone to war with before.

"He's battle-tested," said Jeff Green, who spent the 2020-21 season with Brown in Brooklyn.

Brown has only been in town for a few months but already feels at home. The 26-year-old from Boston is a low-key guy. In Denver, he can live downtown and close to Ball Arena but still enjoy his peace and quiet. It's more his speed than his old borough, Brooklyn.

"Obviously, New York gets a lot of attention, a lot of media attention," Brown said. "That wasn't for me."

"I'm more laid back. I chill."

He's especially close with Green and DeAndre Jordan, who also played for the Nets during the 2020-21 season. At Nuggets training camp in San Diego, Brown and Jordan found a free afternoon to hit the golf course. The two also have a pregame handshake where Brown acts like he's swinging an iron from the fairway while Jordan putts from an imaginary green.

He'll have to wait until the offseason to trim his handicap though. Brown's here to help the Nuggets win a championship this year. If Denver does break through, it's going to be because the Nuggets defend at a championship level. Brown knows he can play a big role in Denver being that last team standing.

"Everybody in this locker room knows what we want," Brown told *DNVR*. "Everybody knows where we want to be at the end of the year." ⌲

The fit for Bruce Brown in Denver was perfect and suited his low-key personality better than his time in Brooklyn.

POWER FORWARD

AARON GORDON

LIVING THE BASKETBALL DREAM IN DENVER

BY **HARRISON WIND** · DECEMBER 14, 2022

This is what Aaron Gordon always wanted.

Gordon's only averaging 10.5 field goal attempts per game this season. It's the fifth-most on the Nuggets and down from the 11.1 Gordon averaged last year. He's not the No. 1, 2 or 3 option in Denver's offense when the Nuggets are at full health. The clutch, late-game, headline-making shots that go viral on Twitter are Nikola Jokic's and Jamal Murray's to take. But that's all good with Gordon. He's more than okay with Denver's current arrangement.

"This is a great brand of basketball," Gordon said. "You play the right way. The open man is the right pass and the right pass is the open man. That's just a beautiful way to play basketball. It reminds me of USA Basketball a little bit and the way that there's energy in the ball and it hops around. It's kind of like FIBA or a world game. It's how I've always wanted to play."

Gordon has found his basketball nirvana in Denver. It's where he's morphed into the perfect winning player and a complementary piece on the Nuggets' contending roster. Gordon's playing a completely different brand of basketball than he did for the first 6 1/2 seasons of his NBA career in Orlando, and this current version of Gordon is almost unrecognizable from the one who played for the Magic.

He's traded in mid-range jumpers for dunks. He's eliminated step-back jump shots from his arsenal and turned his focus to finding open catch-and-shoot triples throughout Denver's offense. He's passing up good shots for great ones that his teammates are attempting. His shooting profile has been refined to a state that fully maximizes the Nuggets' attack.

This season, 62% of Gordon's shots are coming at the rim. His previous career high was only 53%. Only 15% of his shots come from the mid-range. Gordon's previous career low was 23%. He's dunking everything once he gets into the paint too. Gordon's 57 dunks through 26 games are the sixth-most in the NBA. Last year he had 130 dunks total.

It's translated into career highs across the board.

Gordon is shooting a ridiculous 70.1% from two-point range. It's the second-best mark in the NBA (out of players with at least 150 attempts) behind only Nic Claxton (73.5%), who's taken exactly two shots from outside the paint all season. That's higher than the 68.4% Nikola Jokic is shooting from two-point range. It's also higher than Rudy Gobert, Clint Capela and Zion Williamson's two-point percentages.

He's picking and choosing his spots from beyond the arc more carefully too. Gordon's three-point

Aaron Gordon was flying high all season in Denver, as he finally found the ideal fit for his explosive skill set.

attempts are down, but his percentage is up. The 38.5% he's shooting from distance would be a career-high. Overall, he's shooting above 60% from the field for the first time in his career. Gordon has also upped his rebounding. He's doing all the little things.

"I'm just looking to be the glue guy," Gordan said. "Do a little bit of a lot. Filling in where my team needs me. Getting where I fit in and making the game easy for the rest of my teammates."

It's been an impressive mindset and one that Gordon has displayed from Day 1 in Denver. His teammates, specifically Nikola Jokic, have appreciated his approach too. You get the feeling that Jokic has the utmost trust in Gordon right now. You've seen their chemistry in the two-man game develop rapidly over the last 2+ seasons. There's a special synergy between Jokic and Gordon when they play together.

"We kind of have almost a little telepathy going on," said Gordon.

Jokic always looks for Gordon when the latter has a mismatch. If there's a switch and Gordon's sealing his man under the rim, Jokic is going to find him. Gordon has been looking to use his physicality and overpower his matchup whenever the opportunity presents itself this season, and Jokic wants to reward Gordon when he can.

"I think you can see how he's developed," Jokic said of Gordon. "He can play screen and roll. He can play 1-on-1 facing the basket. He can rim-run. He's a complete player. He doesn't have a weak spot."

"He's a top-5 two-way player in the league right now."

Gordon's overall play and night-in-night-out consistency has been an underrated storyline this season. He's unquestionably been the Nuggets' second-best player. If Gordon was averaging a few more points per game — he's currently at 16.7 this year — the forward would be garnering All-Star consideration right now. If the Nuggets are atop the Western Conference when ballots are submitted in a couple of months, he might even grab some votes. Gordon has been that good and is becoming a more dangerous player within the Nuggets' offense by the day.

His overall game has matured too. Gordon is understanding the court and reading the floor at an incredibly high level. He's mastering the art of the dunker spot. He's become elite at floating into the open spaces around the basket that Jokic creates with his gravity. Gordon followed through on his pledge at the conclusion of last season to raise his basketball IQ to better complement the back-to-back MVP, and the basketball knowledge he added over the summer has made him a rock-solid fit next to Jokic and on this roster.

"I think it's more streamlined, the way that I play my game," Gordon said. "A lot of stuff in my bag, but now I just know when to use it, where to use it, and how it's going to affect the game."

His play this season has helped the Nuggets settle in at 16-10 overall and near the top of the West while battling injuries, illnesses and inconsistent play. Jokic and Murray missed time with COVID. Michael Porter Jr. has been sidelined for the last 10 games with a heel strain. Denver's bench has been a work-in-progress to put it kindly. The defense has been a disaster. Gordon, along with most Nuggets players, deserves the blame for that.

But Gordon's offensive consistency and dedication to his role have been fundamental to Denver's success so far. He's playing both the style of basketball that he wants and the one that the Nuggets need him to in order to chase their championship dreams.

"I have another level to get to," Gordon said. "And so does this team." ⊠

Aaron Gordon and Nikola Jokic have developed a great chemistry and two-man game in their limited time as teammates.

'I WAS JUST WATCHING HIM GLIDE'

AARON GORDON'S CHRISTMAS DUNK IS AN ALL-TIME SLAM

BY **HARRISON WIND** · DECEMBER 26, 2022

Think about the circumstances Aaron Gordon was dealing with in overtime.

It was only a one-point game. The Nuggets were clinging to a 124-123 lead with less than 30 seconds on the clock. It was a classic situation where Denver would typically milk the possession. It was one of those points in the game where Nikola Jokic would usually direct everyone into their proper position on the court, conduct the Nuggets' two-man pick-and-roll game from the top of the 3-point arc and leave the Suns with as little time remaining as possible.

Gordon had another idea.

"It was a loose, ball," Gordon said as he began recapping the sequence. "KP caught the rebound, and then it came to me. You can't do take fouls anymore, so I was able to get out around the outside. Then I saw I had a 2-on-1 with me and Joker. You know you've got to play Joker and play a little cat-and-mouse game. As soon as I saw them play that little cat and mouse game and hesitate on who (the defender) was going to go to, I was like, I'm just going to take off."

Gordon's decision to push the issue resulted in the dunk of the year. Considering the situation and the volume of the moment, on national TV on Christmas Day, it was an all-time slam.

Gordon first got past Mikal Bridges at half-court. Then when Landry Shamet didn't commit to him and the ball, Gordon picked up his dribble at the 3-point line, gathered with two feet, and threw down a rim-rocking jam over Shamet that set a sell-out crowd at Ball Arena off.

"He stepped over and kind of like bumped me," Gordon said of Shamet. "And it raised me up a little bit higher."

"I was open," joked Jokic.

"I didn't think he was going to dunk it," said Murray. "It was a 3-on-2 and he didn't show he was going to dunk it. He was just running, and he just jumped."

But then, confusion. Referee Matt Boland called a charge on Gordon. The Nuggets forward stood for a few moments under the basket he had just destroyed dazed and confused.

The crowd was stunned.

The Nuggets were furious.

"I'm thinking it's an and-1," Gordon said afterward.

Luckily, the officials took another look. Denver had already used its challenge, but a little-known rule that allows referees to review a play where the defender may have drawn a charge in the restricted area, as long as it's in the last two minutes of the fourth quarter, gave the dunk new life. Tony Brothers took another look and reversed the ruling.

"That Aaron Gordon dunk was, damn," Michael

Malone said. "I'm just glad they reviewed it and made the right call."

Murray said Gordon's slam reminded him of his 2020, one-handed poster over DJ Wilson that he was whistled for a charge on.

"I was like no way they called an offensive foul," Murray said.

After a short review, the call was overturned, and the basket stood.

Pandemonium ensued.

Ball Arena erupted.

"From my angle, I was watching him just glide," Murray said. "That's crazy. Dunk of the year for sure."

Gordon has had some monster dunks throughout his 10-year NBA career. He'd had some memorable ones in dunk contests too. Gordon has scored eight 50-point dunks in dunk contests. It's the most 50-point dunks of all time. That's one more than both Michael Jordan and Zach LaVine, who both have seven to their name.

Of course, Gordon has never won a dunk contest. It's why he currently wears No. 50, the number that signifies a perfect dunk contest score.

Because of time and score, Gordon believes this was his best-ever in-game slam.

"AG, was that a 50?" Gordon was asked postgame.

"I don't know," he said. "Maybe a 49." ⌧

A WINNING CONNECTION

NUGGETS LOCKER ROOM IN SYNC AND IT SHOWS

BY **HARRISON WIND** · JANUARY 10, 2023

Michael Malone had never seen anything like it.

At halftime of the Nuggets' 31-point blowout win over the Los Angeles Clippers last week, Malone turned on a film edit that highlighted Denver's best defensive plays from the opening two quarters. The Nuggets had just held the Clippers to 32 points on 27% shooting. Kawhi Leonard was shooting 2-7 from the floor. Paul George was 1-9.

Inside the Nuggets' locker room, players clapped as Malone went through Denver's standout defensive possessions from the first half. They cheered as one defensive stop after another played on the big screen. It was a boisterous, raucous halftime atmosphere that Malone wasn't used to. It was the first time in his 30 years of coaching that he had experienced that type of halftime reaction.

"I think it reinforced to our guys that everything we've talked about is right in front of us," Malone said.

The scene that played out in the Nuggets' locker room that night provides a sliver of insight into how locked in Denver is right now. The Nugget beat the LeBron James, Anthony Davis-less Lakers 122-109 at Ball Arena in a game that was never that close. The NBA's best offense didn't have a particularly good night — the Nuggets shot 46% from the field, 36% from three and turned it over 17 times — but it didn't matter. Denver frustrated the Laker offense and eased to its 13th win in 16 games. The Nuggets are now 17-3 at home and tied with the Memphis Grizzlies for the best home record in the NBA.

The word right now that's circulating around the Nuggets is "connected." It's a word that a lot of people within the organization are using to talk about the current state of this team. They're connected on offense. They're connected on defense. Everyone knows their role. Everyone is doing their part. It's a tone that's of course set by Nikola Jokic, who dominated Monday's win while attempting only five shots (he made all five) and finished with a 14-point, 11-rebound, 16-assist triple-double. The Nuggets are playing unselfish basketball. They're playing for each other.

Kentavious Caldwell-Pope, who's new in Denver this season, frequently talks to Nuggets coaches about all the open shots he gets throughout a game even

Jamal Murray, Michael Porter Jr. and Nikola Jokic set the tone in an increasingly successful Denver locker room.

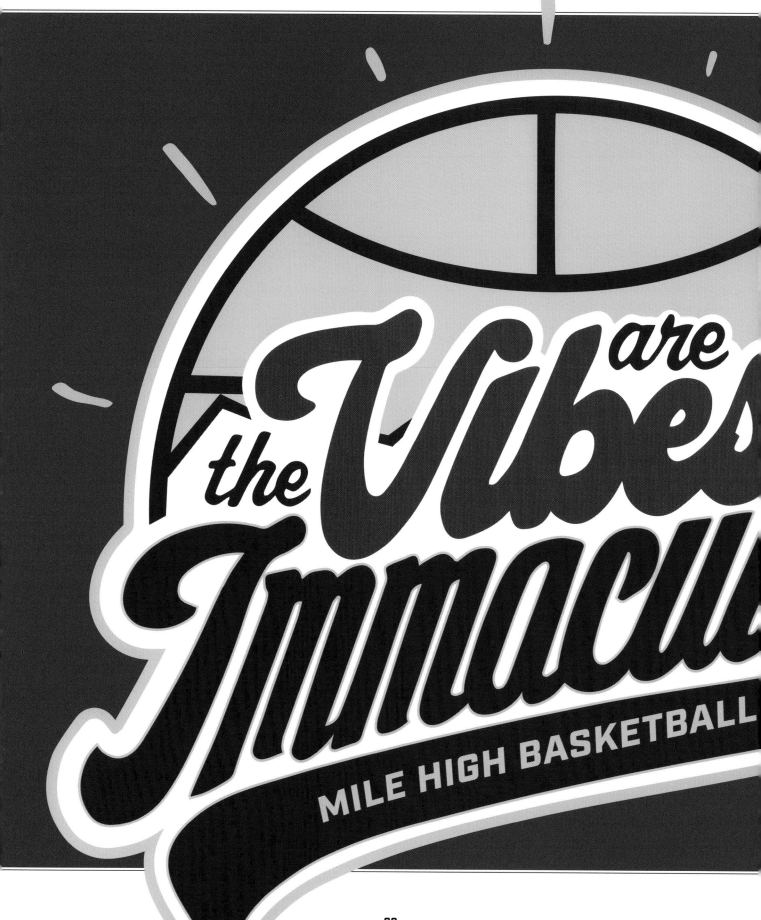

the Vibes are Immacu...

MILE HIGH BASKETBALL

though he doesn't get any plays called for him. He knows that if he does his job, runs the floor, and plays the right way, he'll get his. Caldwell-Pope is in basketball heaven.

It's hard not to get really excited about the Nuggets right now. I've never seen a team score easier than Denver this season. The Nuggets are gradually ramping up defensively too. Denver has the 12th-best defense over its last 15 games. If you look up and down the Western Conference, it's as wide-open as ever. From talking with people around the Nuggets, you gather that the only West team that Denver has any real worry about is the Warriors.

Everything's coming together for the Nuggets, and Jamal Murray's looking more and more comfortable by the game. His play was the most encouraging takeaway from the Nuggets' latest win. Murray went for a season-high 34 points against the Lakers, converted 5-of-9 from 3-point range and tallied seven rebounds, four assists and two steals. He went to the rim with confidence all night. He aggressively attacked the paint when the opportunity presented itself. He played physical defense.

"This was just an all-around Jamal Murray type of a basketball game," said Malone.

Here's another sign that Murray is almost all the way back: He and Dennis Schröder were going at each other Monday night. That matchup got physical on the perimeter and in the post. And Murray was the aggressor. It was one of his best nights of the season, but Murray downplayed his performance afterward.

"I was just playing basketball," he said.

It's a tell that while he's in a real groove right now, Murray knows there's another gear that he and the Nuggets can get to. There's another level they can reach.

As long as the Nuggets stay connected, they'll get there. 🖼

CENTER

NIKOLA JOKIC

WRITING HIS LEGACY

BY **HARRISON WIND** · JANUARY 19, 2023

Nikola Jokic never looks too far into the future. He's the rare NBA superstar who lives in the moment. He operates matchup to matchup and game to game. Jokic is never thinking about what a stat line that's never been posted since Wilt Chamberlain means for his MVP candidacy. He's never been concerned with what another triple-double will do for his standing in NBA history.

But on Wednesday, Jokic reflected for a moment. He took a second to ponder his own legacy, one that's being written in real-time and had a chapter added to it in the Nuggets' latest win.

"I want everybody to remember me as the guy who was a really good team player," Jokic said a couple of hours after he became the Nuggets' all-time franchise leader in assists.

Jokic moved passed Nuggets legend and Hall-of-Famer Alex English atop the franchise's assist leaderboard with 8:44 left in the third quarter of the Nuggets' 122-118 win over the Timberwolves. After a Minnesota turnover, Jokic, like he often has throughout his career, quickly handed the ball to the

closest official, hurried to the sideline and inbounded the ball before the defense was set. He found a wide-open Kentavious Caldwell-Pope behind the defense for Denver's easiest basket of the night.

In classic Jokic fashion, he had no idea he was closing in on the record. Nuggets PR Director Nick O'Hayre informed him earlier this week that he was about to break it. In the postgame locker room, Jokic was presented with the game ball signed by all of his teammates.

"It's not something that I was dreaming of or wanted to achieve," Jokic said.

Jokic is arguably the best scorer in the NBA. He faces constant double-teams and varied defensive schemes every night yet is averaging 25.1 points per game on historical efficiency. He's the most efficient post-up player in the NBA. He can score from anywhere on the floor. But passing has always been his preferred method to dissect a defense.

This is the same guy who proclaimed at the Nike Hoop Summit back in 2017 that basketball "is about teammates," and then announced midway through his

Nikola Jokic is a pass-first player at his core, evidenced by setting the Nuggets' franchise record for assists.

sophomore season that he prefers to pass rather than score because assists "make two people happy."

He never diverted from that philosophy, and the rest of his team has followed his lead.

In the NBA, your best player sets the culture for your entire organization. Ever since Jokic has taken the reigns as Denver's cornerstone and foundation, a selfless style of basketball has spread throughout the Nuggets' locker room. The Jokic way has been contagious. Throughout most of the Jokic era, the Nuggets have always passed up good shots for great ones. Look over to the sideline and you'll always see Denver's reserves, who aren't getting playing time, ecstatic for their teammates who are currently taking their minutes.

That's his legacy.

With every new player that joins the Nuggets' organization, you see Jokic's influence. Last offseason, Aaron Gordon committed to raising his basketball IQ and becoming a smarter overall player so he could better compliment Jokic and play better off of him. Gordon realized that the best way to play was Jokic's way and completely reshaped his game after arriving in Denver. Michael Porter Jr. came into the NBA as a No. 1 scorer and an absolute bucket-getter. Throughout his entire high school career, he was relied on every night to manufacture points, by himself. Now in his fourth season, Porter has completely bought into the Nuggets' unselfish nature. You can't tell me Jokic's basketball philosophy had nothing to do with that.

That's his legacy.

Jokic will likely sit atop every Nuggets leaderboard one day. I'm confident that he'll never seriously think about playing for another franchise. If Jokic continues at this current pace, he'll one day score more points than English did in a Nuggets jersey. He'll

pretty soon secure more rebounds than Dan Issel (Jokic needs only 724 rebounds for that crown). He's already the best player in Nuggets' history and the record books will eventually show it.

But you do get the feeling that this honor means more to him than those will. When a Jokic statue eventually gets built outside of Ball Arena, it should be of Jokic passing. Because that's him. Jokic is an incredible all-time scorer, but making his teammates better is what defines him as a player.

"To be honest, maybe that's the first thing I'm kind of proud of," Jokic said after breaking the record Wednesday night. "Just because hopefully my teammates love to play with me because I share the ball."

That's his legacy. ⌂

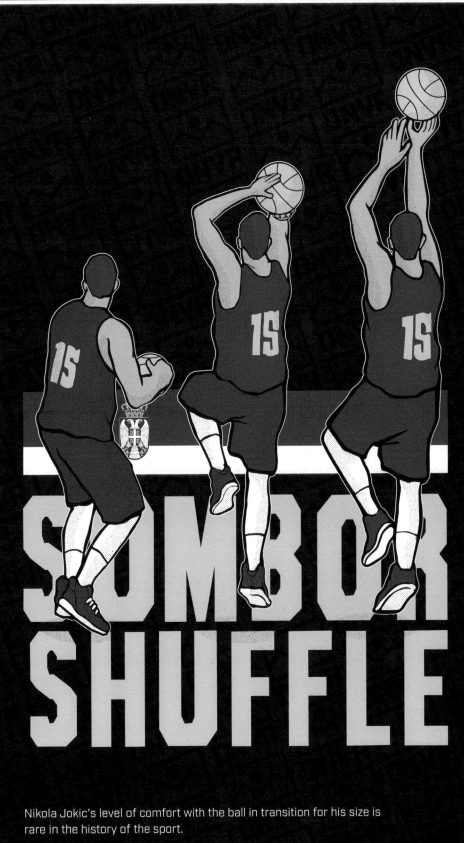

SOMBOR SHUFFLE

Nikola Jokic's level of comfort with the ball in transition for his size is rare in the history of the sport.

A GROWING BOND

HOW THE "TRUST" BETWEEN JAMAL MURRAY, MICHAEL PORTER JR. CONTINUES TO GROW

BY **HARRISON WIND** · FEBRUARY 27, 2023

As soon as the ball left Michael Porter Jr.'s hands, Jamal Murray raised his arms in celebration. He already knew what was about to happen next.

It was the biggest play from the Nuggets' thrilling 134-124 OT win Sunday over the Los Angeles Clippers. After Kawhi Leonard nearly stole the ball away from Murray with the Nuggets down 118-117 and under 40 seconds remaining in the fourth quarter, Murray regained possession and misfired on a half-court prayer as the shot clock expired. But Kentavious Caldwell-Pope corralled what Michael Malone and Caldwell-Pope agreed was the "biggest rebound of his career" and reset the ball to Murray.

With the Clippers' defense scrambling, Murray found a wide-open Porter on the right wing.

Splash.

It was a cold-blooded, no-doubt triple from one of the best pure shooters in the NBA who's also proven to be extremely clutch. This is hardly Porter Jr.'s first high-pressure triple. Who can forget his Game 5 3-pointer against the Clippers — the original "Yeah, Mike!" shot — with 1:11 on the clock and Denver up 102-100? Then there was the double-OT Game 5 corner 3 off the cross-court Nikola Jokic feed against Portland in the 2021 postseason. There have been others too. The kid has ice water in his veins.

That feed in OT against the Clippers also came from Murray, who also found Porter Jr. in transition on the left wing for a massive early-dagger 3-pointer in overtime Sunday.

Murray looked Porter Jr.'s way often against the Clippers. Five of Porter Jr.'s 12 baskets came off Murray assists. It's a result of a growing chemistry between the two.

That chemistry first began to develop off the court last season when Porter Jr. missed most of the year due to another back surgery and Murray missed all of it rehabbing his torn ACL. Murray and Porter Jr. started to hang out more away from the team. They began going to church together. Now, there's more belief in each other between the lines.

"We've developed a bond off the court that's translated on the court," Porter Jr. said Sunday. "We have more trust in each other."

It's a key development in the chemistry and hierarchy within the Nuggets' starting lineup. Too often in past games, we've seen Porter Jr. get hot but then go quiet for stretches of important game action. He could have a "Porter Quarter" and go crazy in the first half, but then become invisible and see his touches evaporate. It's mostly been a product of the Nuggets' selfless nature and having so much offensive talent in their starting lineup and on their roster.

But now Porter Jr. feels that he and Murray's relationship has grown to a level where Murray is making it a point to keep him involved. If a few

While Nikola Jokic's (15) style of play matches up well with just about any teammate, the growing cohesion between Jamal Murray (27) and Michael Porter Jr. (1) unlocked another level to Denver's attack.

possessions go by where Porter Jr. hasn't gotten a touch, Porter Jr. says Murray will call a play for him. If Porter Jr. is hot and isn't getting the ball, Murray now looks to swing it to him even when he and Jokic go into their two-man, pick-and-roll game.

"He makes sure that I don't get iced out," Porter Jr. said. "…He's just very conscious of trying to get me going."

That chemistry led to one of Porter Jr.'s best games of the season Sunday against the Clippers. Porter Jr. finished with 29 points on a clean 12-18 shooting (4-8 3FGs) and 11 rebounds. He didn't just stand beyond the arc and let it fly from deep either. He got out in transition and got to the rim in the half-court too. As Porter Jr. has gotten healthier this season and begun to trust his body more, you're seeing how versatile his offensive game can be even when playing against the NBA's most feared defenses.

"How about some of the drives?" Malone asked postgame. "You're seeing the complete player that he is. He's not just a one-trick pony that can make 3s."

Denver's starting five was already unstoppable. How unguardable the Nuggets are is the biggest reason why Denver is in a prime position to capture its first NBA championship this season. You can't stop Jokic in the playoffs. Caldwell-Pope and Aaron Gordon have carved out roles as the perfect complimentary offensive pieces to the back-to-back MVP. Murray can be a killer in the postseason. We know that.

But Porter Jr. playing at this level turns the Nuggets' offense up even higher. It makes the Nuggets so much tougher to stop. Even the NBA's top defenses don't stand a chance. ⌧

SMALL FORWARD

MICHAEL PORTER JR.

GROWING INTO THE BEST STORY OF THIS NUGGETS' SEASON

BY **HARRISON WIND** · MARCH 7, 2023

A few days ago at Nuggets practice, Michael Malone took Michael Porter Jr. aside to deliver a succinct message: I'm proud of you.

Porter Jr. has met every challenge that the Nuggets coaching staff laid out for him entering this season, and Malone wanted to let the 24-year-old know that his buy-in wasn't going unnoticed. Be a better and more committed defender. Put more effort in on the defensive end of the floor. Trust that the ball will find you in this offense. Be more than just a spot-up 3-point shooter.

Porter Jr. has done it all.

"I think Michael Porter [Jr.] has been just tremendous on both ends of the floor all season long," said Malone after Porter Jr., who played under the weather Monday, tallied 20 points on a clean 7-11 shooting (4-6 3FGs) against Toronto. "That's maturation."

Porter Jr. has gone from a luxury to a necessity on this Nuggets team. Now, late in the regular season, Porter Jr. is a key to what the Nuggets do. Denver counts on him to produce every night and the Nuggets need him at his best in order to reach their championship goals.

You felt that again Monday in the Nuggets' 118-113 win over the Raptors. The Nuggets don't get their 30th win of the season at Ball Arena if Porter Jr. doesn't show up. That's been the case often this year.

It was also Porter Jr.'s fifth 20+ point game across his last seven outings. There's a consistency and reliability to Porter Jr.'s game right now that's never been there before. There's a steadiness to his minutes that you didn't feel in years past. You no longer have to wonder about the impact he's going to make every night. You can now simply pencil Porter Jr. in for a good game. You can assume that he's going to play winning basketball. In the 32 games since Porter Jr. returned from a heel injury in late December that sidelined him for around one month, he's averaging 17.7 points (49.8 FG%, 40.5 3P%) and 5.2 rebounds per game.

He's giving the Nuggets exactly what they need. It's inspiring to think about where Porter Jr.'s at now after three back surgeries, three lengthy rehabs, all the time he's spent away from the court, and the non-basketball family matters he's navigated this year. What a story he's writing.

Michael Porter Jr.'s talent was always elite but the maturation of his game and buy-in to his role on the team raised the ceiling for the Nuggets.

Porter Jr.'s also feeling healthier than he has in a while, and that's reflected in how often he's looking to go to the rim. He's trusting his body and exploring his offensive game. Porter Jr. is so much more comfortable attacking off the dribble now than he was earlier in the year. It feels like there's still another level (or two) that his offensive game can reach.

And then there's his defense, which completes the arc of Porter Jr.'s year and makes his maturation this season arguably the best storyline of this current Nuggets campaign. Porter Jr. has become a fine defender, and he's been a fixture in the Nuggets' starting lineup as Denver has scaled the NBA's defensive ranks. The Nuggets are currently the 12th-best defense in the league and the 5th-best defense since Dec. 7. That's a 41-game sample, or more than half the season so far. Denver has also maintained the best clutch defense in the NBA for most of this year. Porter has been on the floor to close out plenty of narrow Nuggets wins.

"I think it's definitely gotten, better," Porter Jr. told *DNVR* regarding his defense. "I'm going to continue to grow and continue to use my intangibles to be disruptive on that end."

"It's about experience, locking into what the other team does, and effort."

These anticipatory steals have become commonplace for Porter Jr.

His teammates have taken notice. There's an appreciation within the Nuggets locker room for how Porter Jr. has bought in and committed himself to being a better defender. There's a level of respect inside Ball Arena for how he's rounded out his game this season.

Because for the Nuggets to win a championship, everyone, including Porter Jr., knows that he has to be reliable on the defensive end of the floor. He can't be singled out in the playoffs and get taken advantage of. He can't be played off the court. He's too important to this team. Porter Jr. has approached this season with that exact thought in mind.

"When teams try to target him, he's taking that personally, and he's stepping up and stopping them," Aaron Gordon told *DNVR*. "That's big because teams were targeting him last year and they can't do that this year. It just makes us that much more difficult to play against when you've got everyone on the court defending."

"He understands what it means this year, what the moment means this year, and he's really stepped up to the challenge. He's really stepped up to the plate defensively." ⌣

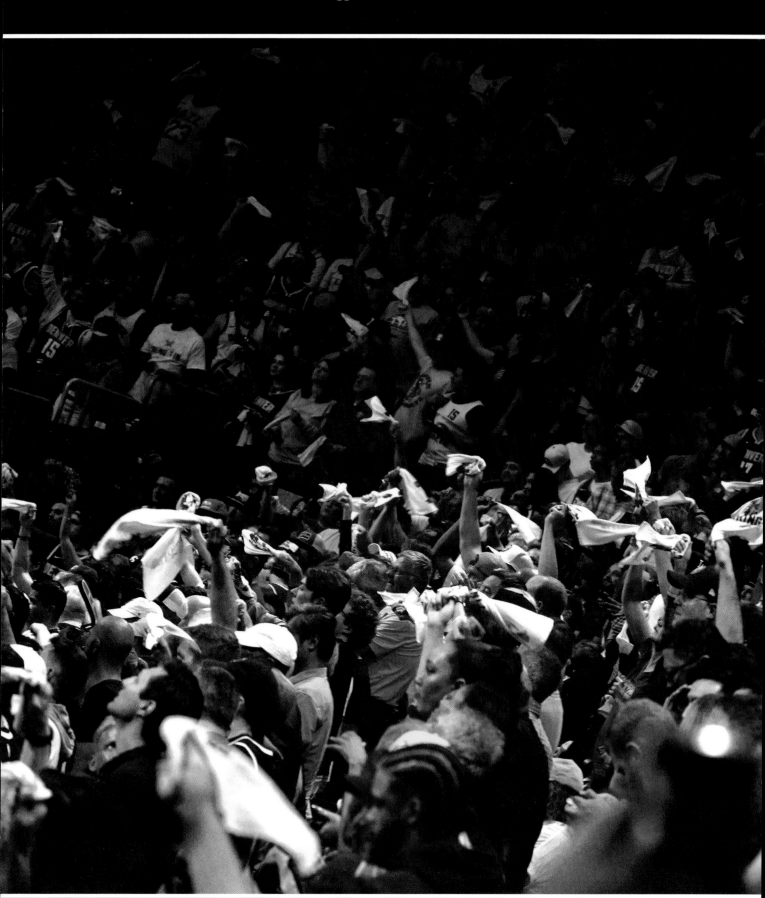

APRIL 16, 2023
DENVER, COLORADO
NUGGETS 109, TIMBERWOLVES 80

DEFENSIVE DOMINANCE

THIS IS WHY THE NUGGETS GOT KENTAVIOUS CALDWELL-POPE

BY **HARRISON WIND**

There's a running joke among the Denver Nuggets coaching staff when it comes to the Defensive Player of the Game Chain, a postgame award given to the player who Michael Malone and his assistants believe was the team's most impactful defender in that night's win.

"He could get the chain every night," Malone said earlier this year about Kentavious Caldwell-Pope. "We should actually name it the KCP DPOG and give it to everybody else."

That's how rock-solid of a defender Caldwell-Pope has been this season. No one on the Nuggets has been steadier this year on the defensive end of the floor than the 10-year veteran who the Nuggets acquired last summer in a trade that made almost too much sense on paper. But for everything that Caldwell-Pope flashed this year across the 76 games he appeared in, it was never really about the regular season with him.

He hit six 3s in an October win over the Thunder. Cool. He went for 20 points in a December victory over the Hornets. Great. He tallied four steals in a January triumph over the Pelicans. Awesome.

With Caldwell-Pope, who's the only current Nuggets player that's won an NBA Championship, it was always about this time of year.

"We didn't get him for the regular season," said Malone.

The Nuggets' 109-80 blowout win over the Minnesota Timberwolves Sunday in Game 1 of their first-round series was the most dominant playoff win over the Nikola Jokic era. Full stop. Denver outscored Minnesota 32-14 in a third quarter for the ages that saw the Timberwolves record more turnovers (6) than made baskets (5). Overall, it was the third-fewest points that the Nuggets have allowed in a playoff game in franchise history.

It was a statement win. It was how a No. 1 seed should look. It was the type of win that can quiet Denver's fiercest doubters for a couple of days, except those who reside on the east coast and didn't stay up on a school night to watch the back-to-back MVP put in work. Nuggets-Timberwolves tipped at approximately 8:50 pm MT.

Per usual, Caldwell-Pope was at the center of the defensive stranglehold Denver put on Minnesota.

He's such a skilled defender when he's guarding one pass away. You rarely see Caldwell-Pope get beat backdoor from the wing.

"Perimeter defensive containment." You've heard Malone recite those three words countless times over the last several years, always out of frustration. Throughout the Jokic era, the Nuggets haven't had a guard that can contain dribble penetration and shut down opposing drivers like Caldwell-Pope can.

This Timberwolves possession ends in a Kyle Anderson 3, but watch the full-court pressure that Caldwell-Pope applies. He gives Mike Conley zero room to breathe.

"It was a stellar defensive performance," Malone

Kentavious Caldwell-Pope set the defensive tone for Denver in the Game 1 win and added 15 points.

said postgame while noting that Sunday's DPOG Chain went to the entire team for the first time this season.

Of course, it could have gone to Caldwell-Pope who recorded a game-high four deflections and held Anthony Edwards, one of his primary assignments, to 6-15 shooting.

And then there's his offense.

After slumping through the Nuggets' post-All-Star break stretch of the season from beyond the arc, Caldwell-Pope returned to form in Game 1. He shot 3-6 from 3-point range and 6-11 from the field overall for 15 points. All three of his made triples came from the corners. Caldwell-Pope was one of six Nuggets players to score in double-figures.

It never feels like Caldwell-Pope is doing too much on offense. He picks his spots carefully. If Denver's offense is on life support — a rare occurrence when Jokic is on the floor — Caldwell-Pope might dribble into and swish a mid-range pull-up. But he's never going to hesitate from 3. In transition, he's composed and calculated. He never looks rushed.

He's a championship-level role player.

"I think he's a very mature player," Michael Porter Jr. said.

It turned out that an experienced, battle-tested, 3-and-D shooting guard was the exact type of player that the Nuggets needed to complete their dream starting five around Jokic. That's who Caldwell-Pope has been throughout his entire career, and acquiring him last offseason felt like an absolute home run deal for Denver at the time.

That's exactly what it's been.

"I don't think there's another dude that you could put alongside us four dudes, me, Aaron, Jamal and Jok that would mold (together) better than us," Porter said of Caldwell-Pope. "It doesn't matter if he gets 12 shots that night, four shots that night, he's going to still play the right way. He's going to make the extra pass. He's going to play defense." ⬚

APRIL 19, 2023
DENVER, COLORADO
NUGGETS 122, TIMBERWOLVES 113

'A WARRIOR'

INSIDE JAMAL MURRAY'S LATEST PLAYOFF EXPLOSION

BY **HARRISON WIND**

You either have it or you don't. You can't learn it. It cannot be taught. It's immeasurable and impossible to quantify.

There's something that's incredibly calming about watching Jamal Murray operate in the highest-leverage moments that the NBA has to offer where he time and time again displays the incalculable intangibles that set him apart from so many of his peers. In the ultimate-stress situations where so many players shrink from the spotlight and fail, Murray time and time again steps up and succeeds. And he does so with a poised and steady mind and a composed, confident, and certain style of play that continually leaves you in awe.

"When the stage is at its biggest, Jamal seems to step up and perform," Michael Malone said after the Nuggets' 122-113 Game 2 win over the Minnesota Timberwolves. "It speaks to his mental toughness, his preparation, his physical toughness, and not being afraid of the moment."

If you were lucky enough to be in attendance Wednesday night at Ball Arena, you witnessed a vintage Murray postseason performance. It was another playoff classic from the 26-year-old who's earning a reputation as one of the NBA's great postseason acts.

40 points on 13-22 shooting, (6-10 from 3-point range), 3 rebounds, 5 assists, 2 steals in 39 minutes.

It was Murray's fifth-career 40-point game in the playoffs. He now has the most 40-point games in Nuggets playoff history.

"Honestly, he lives for the playoffs," Michael Porter Jr. said. "He lives for moments like these."

Murray's night was fairly consistent. He erupted for 14 points in the first quarter, capitalizing on a Timberwolves' starting lineup change that swapped Nickeil Alexander-Walker, who defended Murray well in Game 1, for veteran Taurean Prince. Murray then went quiet with only four points in the second before tallying 12 in the third. Murray hit double-digits again in the fourth quarter, scoring 10 points in the period and eight of the Nuggets' final 14 points of regulation.

Step-back triples, pull-up jumpers, ISO fadeaway daggers. It was the full Murray repertoire and featured some incredible shot-making.

The Nuggets needed Murray's 40-piece. Anthony Edwards, who went off for 41 points of his own Wednesday, kept the Timberwolves in Game 2. Minnesota outscored Denver 40-23 in the third quarter to erase the Nuggets' 20-point first-half lead, but Murray and the Nuggets proved in the fourth that they were just the better side.

By the time the final buzzer sounded, Murray was absolutely spent. Before he subbed out to a standing

Jamal Murray went off with 40 points and six three-pointers in the Game 2 win over the Timberwolves.

Aaron Gordon finishes with authority as Rudy Gobert looks on. Gordon had 12 points and 10 rebounds as the Nuggets took control of the series.

ovation with 11 seconds left on the clock, Murray stood at the foul line closest to the Nuggets' bench during a break in the action with his hands on his knees. It looked like he was gasping for air.

"That kid is a warrior," Malone said.

"He left a piece of him out there tonight."

Murray knew heading into the playoffs that it would take him a minute — or maybe just one game — to find his real rhythm. In Game 1 and in Murray's first playoff game in two years, the emotions were flowing. He was maybe too amped up and too excited. But entering Game 2, Murray was more relaxed and composed. He felt more like his typical postseason self.

His teammates sense that Murray's back and even better than ever. Earlier this week, Michel Porter Jr. said he believes that Murray is a better player now than he was before tearing his ACL at the end of the 2021 regular season. Following Game 2, Nikola Jokic echoed the same sentiment.

"I think he's playing now better than in the bubble," Jokic said. "Yes, he scored a lot more points in the bubble, or whatever, but I think his energy is much better. His leadership, his — not focus — just like being into the game, it's at a much higher level I think now."

**

There's another angle to Murray's latest playoff banger — one that extends well beyond last night and will pave the way for the next chapter of his basketball story.

We all know that Murray is trying to get back to the player he was pre-ACL injury. We've had discussions all year about whether he's back or not and what Murray being back actually looks like. Murray was asked by *DNVR* Wednesday if in Game 2 he felt anything similar to what he felt during the 2020 playoffs, in the bubble and in some of those games where he dropped 40, even 50 points.

"I don't think the bubble and Jamal — we're the same person — I'm not split," Murray responded. "I'm kind of exhausted of hearing about that person like that's not me. That was just the beginning in my opinion. I have to keep my mentality that way. If I keep looking back like you guys and think that was it, I'm not going to exceed that. I look at that as if that was the beginning. And I'm 26. I have a lot of career left, hopefully, god-willing. So I want to keep getting better, keep trending. That's my mindset."

He later expounded on the Bubble Murray comparisons following Game 2.

"You can reference it for sure, but it's not two different people. I'm working to get myself back to that level and better and beyond. I don't want to listen to everybody thinking that that was it. There's more to come. There's better performances to come. There's a better mentality. There's a healthier body. There's an offseason where I can train. There's a lot of different factors. It's a mentality for me. I have to say it. I have to be about it and I have to believe it. And hopefully, you guys believe it too."

It was a profound response. Murray is done hearing about comparisons to the player he was in the 2020 playoffs. He knows he can get back to that level

— Porter even said following Game 2 that the Murray he watched play on Wednesday was "exactly" like the Murray he watched in the bubble — and eventually exceed it. And he doesn't want that playoff run to define him as a player, even though right now it of course does. He knows there's more in the tank. He wants to ultimately rise to a higher level. The player he was in the bubble isn't this mythical person. He's right here. Jamal Murray is here.

"The bubble was just weird because there were no fans," Porter said. "This is even more special."

Murray is well on his way to firmly establishing himself as one of the best postseason performers in the NBA. He already has the second-highest percentage of career playoff games in NBA history where he scores 40+ points, trailing only Michael Jordan. He's a prime-time player, an absolute killer in the clutch, and a force that you want to go to war behind. You can believe in Jamal Murray.

It feels like everything is on the table now, including the opportunity that Murray wants — the chance for him to break free from the bubble Murray comparisons for good.

What would then define Murray's career going forward? Maybe it's what's about to happen in these playoffs. ⌧

STAR SPOTLIGHT BY BRENDAN VOGT
JAMAL MURRAY – A+

Jamal Murray turned in two of the best performances of his career Wednesday night. The first came on the court — his first playoff masterpiece in front of a friendly home crowd in years. He's done it on the road, and he's done it in the bubble, a word we're all sick of by now.

Murray tore the wolves to shreds to the tune of 40 points. He was ferocious, yet not at the cost of grace. We've seen this so many times in the playoffs. The occasionally labored dribbling in the regular season is supplanted by mesmerizing footwork and stunning confidence. By the time he was done

scoring Wednesday night, he'd erased any doubt in his capability of replicating his past accomplishments. And that's sincerely important to him.

"You can reference the bubble," Murray told the media after the game. "(But) it's not two different people...I'm kind of exhausted of hearing (about) that person," he elaborated. "That's not me. That's just the beginning...I have to keep my mentality that way. If I keep looking back, as you guys think, that was it — I'm not going to exceed that."

APRIL 21, 2023
MINNEAPOLIS, MINNESOTA
NUGGETS 120, TIMBERWOLVES 111

SILENCING THE CROWD

THE NUGGETS ARE PROVING THEY'RE EVERYTHING THE TIMBERWOLVES ARE NOT

BY **HARRISON WIND**

The decibel level at Target Center reached what felt like a new Game 3 high after an Anthony Edwards 3-pointer that pulled the Timberwolves to within three points of the Nuggets with 10:32 left in the fourth quarter.

Then three minutes later, it reached a new low.

That's how quickly everything changes in the playoffs. That's how quickly a game can flip. Minnesota was building momentum during an early fourth-quarter run. The crowd was back. The belief was there, I think.

Christian Braun quickly snatched it all away.

The rookie was the catalyst of a 9-2 Nuggets burst immediately following Edwards' triple that helped Denver to a 120-111 win in Game 3 Friday night. Braun had three layups — including one that went over/through Timberwolves shot-blocker Rudy Gobert — and a key assist that led to a Michael Porter Jr. 3 during the run.

"He's just poised, and you need a certain level of poise to be playing this time of year," Aaron Gordon said of Brown.

"We're very lucky to have him," added Porter.

Target Center turned dead silent after Braun's fourth-quarter explosion. The in-arena MCs tried to rile the Timberwolves faithful back up but to no avail. The building was dead. Timberwolves fans were done. This series feels like it's finished.

After the win, *DNVR* asked Braun what it's like to quiet an entire opposing arena on this stage.

He gave the response of a 10-year vet.

"Just trying to get any lead that we could, to get our guys back in there," Braun said. "To get that lead back, especially after I made that mistake, it obviously felt good. When I do make opportunities, I've got to make the most of them."

The mistake Braun is referring to was an early-fourth quarter turnover that preceded Edwards' 3. For a moment, the always-poised rookie looked a little rattled. No one would have blamed him either. This is a big stage, and Target Center can reach a level of loud that I'm not sure Ball Arena can — not because of the fans in either building but due to how it's constructed and how old the Timberwolves' arena is. It's just a different kind of noise and roar here.

But Malone stuck with Braun and it paid off.

"If I yank Christian Braun out after a turnover, how is he going to be able to impact the game?" Malone said. "He's going to be looking over his shoulder after every mistake. You can't play like that."

Denver's Game 3 win should put the end to this series in sight. And by now, you can see a stark contrast between these two teams.

The Nuggets play together. They play for each other. They're an actual team. The Timberwolves give off the vibe that they aren't.

"Our team is not just Nikola," Malone said. "It's not just Jamal."

Denver has maturity, leadership, chemistry, culture, poise and execution. The Nuggets play for each other. They pick one another up. They're selfless. A lot of times those can be hallow words, but in this case they aren't.

The Nuggets are everything the Timberwolves are not. And that has been extremely apparent through three games.

What's also been clear so far in this series is that the Nuggets seem like they're on a mission. They haven't gotten too high or too low after any of these three wins. This has been a very business-like approach.

"The focus that we've had, and our discipline has been off the charts," said Nikola Jokic after he recorded the NBA's first triple-double of the playoffs in Game 3, a 20-point, 11-rebound, 12-assist effort.

Denver talked a big game at practice all week leading into this series about how locked in and focused they were. This team wasn't lying one bit. The Nuggets expected to dominate and have dominated.

They should again in Game 4. 🖼

STAR SPOTLIGHT BY BRENDAN VOGT
MICHAEL PORTER JR. - A

The story of round one so far is one of maturation. The Nuggets look older, wiser, and better prepared than ever for a deep postseason run. At the heart of that is the maturation of Michael Porter Jr. A once awkward fit in the organization has become the poster boy for their thriving culture. He's embraced the expectations, his teammates have embraced him, and now the Wolves are on the wrong end of a brilliant narrative.

Porter's blossomed into a bonafide third option on a genuine contender. He's making an impact in all the areas expected of him. He's defending well, inhaling rebounds, and breaking the dam offensively. Much like Klay Thompson, perhaps Porter's most frequent and apt comparison, his buckets take all the air out of the building. Jamal Murray and Nikola Jokic were hard enough to stop. With a third star fully integrated, the Wolves' actual opponent in this series is futility. How long will they rage against the inevitable? That's all they can do while Porter's playing at this level.

APRIL 23, 2023
MINNEAPOLIS, MINNESOTA
TIMBERWOLVES 114, NUGGETS 108 (OT)

NOT SO SMOOTH SAILING

HOW NICKEIL ALEXANDER-WALKER EMERGED AS THE DEFENSIVE X-FACTOR IN NUGGETS-TIMBERWOLVES

BY **HARRISON WIND**

The Nuggets' 114-108 Game 4 overtime loss can be boiled down to a few major talking points.

- Nuggets players not named Nikola Jokic shot 27-68 (39.7%) from the floor.
- Denver got out-rebounded 51-47 and gave up 14 offensive rebounds.
- The Nuggets did not shoot well from 3-point range — 12-35 (34.3%) as a team. Several of those makes came late in the game too.
- In overtime, the Timberwolves shot 6-8 overall and 4-6 from 3-point range.
- Jamal Murray scored 19 points on just 8-21 (38.1%) shooting

Let's focus in on that last bullet point.

You can't put this loss solely on Murray's shoulders, but a better shooting game from him and Denver would have been in a better position Sunday night to sweep the series. Murray also shot 1-8 from the floor in the second half but did have two buckets in overtime — one sweeping layup around Rudy Gobert and a breakaway layup off a Jokic Hail Mary.

One reason for Murray's struggles was the presence of Nickeil Alexander-Walker, who has emerged as the Timberwolves' defensive X-factor and was in the starting lineup again for Minnesota in Game 4. He was the primary matchup on Murray

and held the Nuggets guard under 20 points for the second-straight game. Murray's point total isn't always a great representation of how well a defender guards him — just because of the number of Nuggets players who can typically put up points — but in Game 4 it was.

Of note on Alexander-Walker…He's 6-5 1/2 with a 6-9 wingspan and is known for his defense. He locked down Shai Gilgeous-Alexander, who's also his cousin, in the Timberwolves' play-in victory over the Thunder to get Minnesota into the playoffs, and he's guarded Murray way more than any other Timberwolves defender in this series. He's also Canadian, like Murray. Alexander-Walker is from Toronto, which is around an hour east of Murray's hometown of Kitchener. He knows Murray's game well.

Murray is shooting 6-27 this series and has turned the ball over five times when guarded by Alexander-Walker, per NBA.com tracking data. That data isn't perfect, and I think it paints the picture that Murray has been bothered by Alexander-Walker more than he actually has been. But Alexander-Walker's defense has been effective.

The Timberwolves certainly think so.

"Nickeil Alexander-Walker has gorilla nuts."

That's what was picked up on a microphone during Alexander-Walker's postgame interview in the Timberwolves locker room after Game 4, courtesy

Although Nikola Jokic dropped 43 points, Nickeil Alexander-Walker's (middle) defense helped frustrate the Nuggets as the Timberwolves prevailed in overtime.

of Anthony Edwards — I think that praise also had a lot to do with Alexander-Walker, who's not an intimidating 3-point shooter even though he's now converted on 43.8% of his 3s this series, dropping in two back-breaking triples from the left corner in overtime of Game 4.

There are ways to counter Alexander-Walker, and freeing Murray up more in Game 5 is an adjustment I'm expecting Denver to make. That's what Michael Malone hinted at in his postgame comments.

"Give him credit. He's done a really good job," Michael Malone said of Alexander-Walker after Game 4. "He's had a harassing, hounding — we've got to look to set screens for Jamal earlier, maybe in the back court, free him up, get him some momentum up the floor, and even get the ball out of Jamal's hands so he's not fighting that for 94-feet every possession, because that can really wear you down. As well as maybe getting a secondary ball handler out there with him."

I'd look for a steady amount of ball screens to be set for Murray near half-court to free him from Alexander-Walker in Game 5. The Nuggets tried it on this possession in Game 2 — and it worked — but Murray wasn't prepared for how high up the floor Kyle Anderson was playing. He'll have to anticipate that going forward in the series.

Malone also mentioned that the Nuggets may look to get another ball-handler on the floor with Murray to get him playing off the ball. Murray has already been logging minutes with Bruce Brown on the second unit, and I'd expect that to continue. Maybe he plays more with Brown?

Malone wouldn't throw Reggie Jackson out there at this point in the series, right? That feels like a massive overreaction to one playoff loss. I also doubt Jackson would really help that much.

It's not like Murray has been totally shut-out while guarded by Alexander-Walker in this series either. He's scored on him 1-on-1 and the Nuggets have been successful screening for Murray and getting another defender switched onto him at times. Murray also has a 40-point game in this series. It was in Game 2 — the one game Alexander-Walker didn't start for Minnesota — but he still logged several possessions where he guarded Murray.

The Nuggets should close out the Timberwolves in Game 5 on Tuesday, but there are adjustments to be made. Let's see what Denver comes up with.

Because one more Murray Flurry and this series will be over. ⊡

Western Conference Quarterfinals, Game 5

APRIL 25, 2023
DENVER, COLORADO
NUGGETS 112, TIMBERWOLVES 109

ARM IN ARM

NUGGETS MAKING HISTORY IN THEIR MARCH THROUGH THE PLAYOFFS

BY **MIKE OLSON**

"Thus, arm in arm with thee, I dare defy my century into the lists." — Friedrich Schiller

When Alex English came to the Denver Nuggets in 1979 as a part of a trade for George McGinnis, there were mixed reviews on the swap. McGinnis had been a long-time star in the league, especially in Indiana who was thrilled to be getting him back, whereas English had only shown promise when given the odd chance with the Bucks and then Pacers.

The trade ended up being a real steal for the Nuggets, where English immediately added nearly six points a game for the Nuggets to the rest of that campaign. While McGinnis' star was descending rapidly, English was a star on the rise. By the next season, the team's strong abilities were clear, but that still wasn't turning into wins. The organization thought maybe a different voice in charge might turn the tide and made Doug Moe the head coach a little over a third into the season. Moe's passion and straightforward words and approach turned out to be just the firebrand the team had needed. Between Doug and Alex, the leading scorer of the next decade, it was a marriage made in heaven.

For the next nine seasons, Moe and English (and Dan Issel and Fat Lever and dozens of others who came in and out of the picture along the way) stayed arm in arm to consecutive playoff appearances, the most memorable of which was probably the team's 1984-85 run to the Western Conference Finals before losing in five game to the Lakers. And while early playoff exits were a critique of the Moe/English-led years, the pair were both able to aggregate a total of 24 wins between them, a record for a player and coach each for the franchise.

It made it somewhat poetic that when they left, both gents were gone from the team in the same offseason. It would be four years before the Nuggets even saw the postseason again, this time with Issel as their coach. That record — 24 playoff wins each — as a player for English, and as a coach for Moe, would stand for another 33 years. Actually, 35, since Moe and English didn't add any wins in their last two postseason appearances together.

When Michael Malone joined the Denver Nuggets as their head coach, he'd had a similarly scant amount of head coaching experience as Moe. In another similarity to Moe, his soon-to-be-star was an even lesser-known quantity.

Nikola Jokic was stunning the coaches and his fellow Nuggets players on the practice court well before his talents were seen by the rest of us, but

Nikola Jokic dominated the Timberwolves with 28 points, 17 rebounds and 12 assists as Denver sent Minnesota fishing with a 4-1 series win.

Malone saw many intangibles falling together for the team when his soft-spoken center steered the offense. Mike took the giant leap of faith that only years later feels like such a no-brainer and handed the reins of the team over to Jokic. With the stellar assistance of players along the way like Jamal Murray, Michael Porter, Jr. and a host of others, Malone and Jokic have cleared one more bar in their quest to bring Nuggets fans the ultimate prize.

With their gentleman's sweep of the Minnesota Timberwolves, both Malone and Jokic notched their 25th playoff wins as head coach and player, smashing the records of Moe and English in a few different ways. Consider the following:

- Jokic and Malone caught that 25th win at the end of a successful series early in their fifth season

- As noted above, English and Moe didn't add a single playoff win to their tallies in their last two seasons with the club, but they still had nine to form that total

- Those paces are even better reflected in their playoff winning clips (Moe/English – .393, Malone/Jokic – .472)

- Each pairing has a Western Conference Finals appearance to point to, with Moe/English losing it to the Lakers in five, and Malone/Jokic losing it to the Lakers in six. (actually, the Melo WCF team also lost it to the Lakers in six. F–the Lakers.)

- You'd have to assume Jokic and Malone will be adding a few more W's into this stat before moving on from these Nuggets. Please let's just go ahead and assume that.

There's been something nearly bromantic about the fact that Jokic and Malone have been able to build this program together, not ignoring the incredible impacts and contributions of dozens of others along the way. But when we get miles and leagues away from this story down the road, and some other young Nuggets hotshot and his coach are being compared to this era, the faces that will be linked together in the successes will be (at least) those of Jokic and Malone. To paraphrase Schiller, when their era/century is compared to those others on the Denver Nuggets list, it may very well defy all the others with its sparkle and glow.

However the playoffs go, however the near-term future of Nuggets basketball goes, that future looks exceedingly bright with Malone and Jokic taking each advent of it together… much like English and Moe did, arm in arm. 🖼

Michael Porter Jr. punches home two of his modest eight points, but also added 10 rebounds in the definitive win over the T-Wolves.

Western Conference Semifinals, Game 1

APRIL 29, 2023
DENVER, COLORADO
NUGGETS 125, SUNS 107

'WE'RE READY FOR THIS'

JAMAL MURRAY SENDS THE SUNS AND THE NUGGETS' SKEPTICS A MESSAGE

BY **HARRISON WIND**

Chris Paul tried to send a message late in the fourth quarter of Saturday's Game 1 between the Nuggets and Suns. His very intentional and borderline dirty shoulder check to Jamal Murray's right side was theoretically supposed to be a reminder, a notice, a warning that would stick in the back of Denver's mind heading into Game 2.

The only problem with Paul's message was that it came too late. Jamal Murray had already delivered a more powerful, potent, and professional one 60 seconds earlier.

"We're ready for this. We've been waiting for this."

The Nuggets' 125-107 Game 1 win was a lot of things. It was a vintage Denver team win that saw six different teammates score in double-figures. It was another strong showing from the Nuggets' bench. It was a lights-out 3-point shooting performance — the Nuggets shot 16-37 (43.2%) — on a night where the Suns only went 7-23 from distance.

But most of all it was a statement win. It was the Nuggets telling the Suns and the rest of the NBA that like Murray said, they're been waiting for this.

Kevin Durant? Devin Booker? Paul? Phoenix, who entering the playoffs was the favorite in the West? Denver isn't intimidated, fazed, or the least bit scared.

A Game 1 blowout may have surprised everyone who tuned in to watch Nuggets-Suns. But it didn't surprise the players in the Nuggets' locker room. This is what the Nuggets expected out of themselves after what they've already accomplished this season.

And they're pissed that no one else saw it coming.

"We know what we're capable of. We're confident in what we can do. We're confident in what we do," Murray said after a dominant 34-point, nine-assist Game 1. "I'm tired of trying to defend ourselves up here like we haven't been playing at this level all season. We're going to keep doing what we're doing and proving everybody wrong."

That quote right there is a peek into the mindset that Murray's operating with right now. Quite frankly, he's playing this postseason with a massive chip on his shoulder. He sat back and took inventory of every negative narrative and take that was uttered about this team and him over the course of this season. Now, he's using it as motivation.

Privately, Murray was ticked off about the first-round playoff storyline that Nickeil Alexander-Walker was bothering him defensively. It fueled him. And by the end of the Timberwolves series, Murray had buried that talking point. Throughout the entire season, Murray has been annoyed by the constant

Jamal Murray was on fire in Game 1, dropping 34 points on 6-of-10 shooting from deep, and adding nine assists.

Nikola Jokic had his way with the Suns in Game 1 with 24 points, 19 rebounds and five assists in the comfortable win.

comparisons of this version of himself to the one that showed up in the 2020 playoffs. He viewed it as everyone putting a ceiling on the player he could get back to and that the guy who balled out in the bubble was some mythical, imaginary person. All of that conversation pissed him off.

He brought that same energy into Round 2.

"It says something to ya'll. We know what we're capable of," Murray said in response to a question about if Denver's Game 1 performance told the Nuggets anything about themselves. "You act like you're surprised."

He channeled it into a brilliant Game 1 performance that you could see coming if you observed Murray prior to tip-off. Murray took the floor for pregame warmups locked in and focused. Typically, Murray's joking around with Aaron Gordon — who he shares a warmup slot with — and has a light-hearted nature about him during that time. But

not before Game 1. He barely cracked a smile during his shooting session.

Murray kept that same all-business approach once the first quarter started. It was immediately clear that he was out for blood Sunday. He paced Denver with 10 first-quarter points. Murray had nine in the second quarter, 10 in the third, and another 10 in a fourth quarter where he drilled one heart-stopping shot after another. Every time that Phoenix went on a run, Murray stopped it in its tracks like he's done so many times already in his playoff career.

He put on a jaw-dropping performance in front of a sold-out Ball Arena crowd that erupted at every one of his makes. Murray preyed on the Suns' defense. He hunted Paul in the pick-and-roll. He might have made Landry Shamet unplayable for the rest of the series. He smirked at how Phoenix chose to guard him and took it as an insult. He wanted all the smoke.

"Those moments, you dream of as a kid," Murray

said. "You try to reenact those in the backyard. Just counting down, or feeling the energy, or hitting a big shot and hearing the crowd that loud, you live for those moments and you want to make the most of those moments. I've been waiting for a while to be healthy and be back and playing at this level at this time of year. It just felt good to feel it."

They say in the NBA that every team takes on the personality of their best player. Throughout the entire Jokic era, the Nuggets have embodied the back-to-back MVP's spirit and selfless nature. This is an unselfish team-first organization because that's who Jokic is. The Nuggets never care who gets the credit and recognition because those are principles that Jokic stands for.

But maybe in the playoffs, this team shifts more toward Murray's mindset because the Nuggets look like they're in a total 'F U' mode right now. They're all playing with Murray's fire and passion. They're all playing like they're pissed off. Everyone's falling in line behind him.

"He's our best player and we are following him right now," Jokic said. "He's bringing the energy, he's bringing the toughness. Everybody's following him."

The Nuggets know this series is just getting started and that the Suns, with Durant, Booker, and Paul are too talented of a team to go down like this. Denver believes Phoenix will adjust and punch back and the Nuggets will try to anticipate the Suns' Game 2 counter-strike as well as possible. As Murray walked off the floor after Game 1, he held up three fingers to the crowd signaling that Denver still has three more games to win.

Who knows how this series will turn out — although you have to feel some type of way about the Nuggets' chances after that Game 1 — but I can guarantee you this: The Nuggets aren't going to be pushed around by the Suns. Denver's going to be the aggressor.

That's unfortunate news for Paul and Phoenix because they clearly wanted to play that role. Paul wants to bully the Nuggets. He wanted to bully Murray and send some sort of lasting message with that fourth-quarter cheap shot that I guess he thought would linger and be something that the Nuggets would be thinking about in the lead-up to Monday's Game 2.

But the problem is that Paul played right into the Nuggets and Murray's hands. It only gave Denver more confidence and belief.

"If he's doing that," Murray said. "Then we're doing something right." 🖂

STAR SPOTLIGHT BY BRENDAN VOGT
JAMAL MURRAY – A+

If only the Nuggets had Jamal Murray, indeed. Murray returned to the Suns — Nuggets matchup and picked up right where he left off against his favorite opponent. So much has changed on either side of the fence since 27 was last involved, and the Nuggets have spent the week denying any notions of revenge. They can and should say that. I don't believe it for one second regarding Murray.

Murray was also excellent defensively, digging deep despite his monster workload. He fed off the crowd all night. The crowd fed off him. It's a beautiful relationship when Denver's cruising at home.

"I don't know how many times I gotta prove myself for y'all to believe in my game," he told TNT after the game. And he hadn't simmered down when he spoke to the rest of the media at the podium. It's a good sign. Murray's too deep in the zone to be tethered to reality regarding feedback. He'll take the disrespect from the national media, manufacture it from the local media if he has to, and turn it all into fuel for the fire. Get out of his way or get torched.

Western Conference Semifinals, Game 2

MAY 1, 2023
DENVER, COLORADO
NUGGETS 97, SUNS 87

NEVER SCARED

AARON GORDON AND THE NUGGETS ARE DOING THE IMPOSSIBLE

BY **HARRISON WIND**

After holding Kevin Durant to 24 points on 10-27 shooting in the Nuggets' 97-87 Game 2 win over the Suns, Aaron Gordon was asked how he was able to find success while guarding the two-time Finals MVP.

But Gordon didn't want to take too much credit for shutting down the player who he called postgame one of the "best scorers of all-time." In classic, selfless Nuggets fashion, Gordon credited his entire team.

"It was really good team defense, honestly," Gordon said. "He was missing shots as well. I was just trying to take away his strengths, contest everything, just contest as much as you can, try to have him shoot over a hand every time."

Denver got defensive contributions from Kentavious Caldwell-Pope and Christian Braun on Durant as well, but Gordon's defense on Durant in Game 2 will go down as his best individual defensive game in a Nuggets uniform to date. Gordon swallowed Durant Monday night at Ball Arena. He didn't let him breathe. He held Durant to his lowest total or the playoff so far. Gordon was in his hip pocket all night.

"I love defense," Gordon said. "I like that aspect of the game. I came into the league as a defender. I feel like there's no other way to play other than to play two ways."

Game 2 was one of the elite playoff defensive performances of the Nikola Jokic-Michael Malone era. The Suns, who entered Game 2 as the best offense in the playoffs, shot just 40% from the field and 6-31 (19.4%) from 3. Gordon, who's been the Nuggets' unsung hero of the playoffs so far, continued to rise to the moment. His defense pretty much took Karl-Anthony Towns out of the Nuggets-Timberwolves first-round series. Gordon already has his fingerprints all over this series as well.

After watching Phoenix in these last two games, I'm not sure the Suns were ready for this type of physicality in Round 2. They certainly don't look like they were expecting Denver to play defense like this. In Game 1, the Nuggets beat the Suns everywhere — in the half-court, in transition, and on the glass — and held Phoenix to 107 points. In a Game 2 where both offenses struggled, Denver dug in defensively and

Aaron Gordon made life hard on Kevin Durant, forcing him into 10-of-27 shooting from the field, including only 2-of-12 from deep.

The Suns had no answer for Nikola Jokic, as he controlled the game with 39 points, 16 rebounds and five assists.

put the clamps on an offensive attack that no one, absolutely no one, thought the Nuggets had a prayer of stopping entering this series.

The Nuggets have now held the Suns to their two lowest-scoring games of the playoffs.

The theme of both of these Nuggets wins is that Denver has been the more physical team. The Nuggets have pushed the Suns around. They've been punking them so far. And slowly but surely, we're discovering what we thought we might know about the Suns entering this series. They don't want to play a physical game. They don't want to bang on the glass. They're a soft, finesse team and the Nuggets are taking advantage.

In Game 1, Chris Paul, who left Game 2 in the second half with groin tightness, was getting beat by Jamal Murray so badly that he retaliated by shoulder-checking Murray on a fast break in the fourth quarter with the game pretty much out of reach. In Game 2,

Devin Booker went chest-to-chest with Bruce Brown after grabbing his jersey and then shoving him during a Nuggets defensive possession. Brown shoved Booker back and then walked away. Gordon and Jamal Murray just stared him down, smiled and smirked.

The Nuggets aren't intimidated by the Suns. They're not scared of this team at all.

The Nuggets currently have the 4th-best playoff defense. Denver has held its opponent under 90 points in now two different playoff games — Game 1 against the Timberwolves and Game 2 against the Suns. The Nuggets are a physical, in-your-face, aggressive defense that now knows it can win in the postseason with its effort on that end of the floor.

Denver has been relying on its defense in the postseason. It's a style that Calvin Booth envisioned when he tweaked this roster last summer and acquired three players — Caldwell-Pope, Brown and Braun — that are playing key defensive roles along with Gordon in these playoffs. The Nuggets' defense on both Durant and Booker has been exceptional in this series.

"Everybody needs to be thankful for them for how aggressive they are and how tough they're playing," said Jokic, who carried the Nuggets' offense in Game 2 with a 39-point, 16-rebound, five-assist masterpiece. "They're making every shot a tough shot."

For as physical as the Nuggets have played in Games 1 and 2, Gordon thinks there's another level they can get to. He wants the Nuggets to take more charges. He also noted after Game 2 that the Nuggets allowed the Suns to collect 11 offensive rebounds. That's something Denver has to clean up ahead of Friday's Game 3 in Phoenix. Gordon wants the Nuggets to crash their offensive glass more too. Denver tallied only five offensive rebounds in Game 2 after finishing with 16 in Game 1.

But the mindset and mission that the Nuggets entered this series with have been on point. The Nuggets are tougher than the Suns. They're the more physical side. They've been more aggressive. They're grittier and more battle tested. So far, this series has been about the Nuggets, a team that has chemistry, culture, trust, and a core that's been through the wars together against the Suns, a team full of individual talents that was put together at this season's trade deadline.

There's a stark difference between these two teams, and that's been crystal clear.

"When you have two evenly matched teams," Malone said. "The more aggressive team is going to win every night." 🖼

STAR SPOTLIGHT BY BRENDAN VOGT
AARON GORDON – A+

Game Two was Aaron Gordon's best game as a Denver Nugget. Had Kevin Durant turned in an excellent performance, the Nuggets could be looking at a 1-1 series heading back to Phoenix. Denver won a dogfight Monday night. And AG was the meanest one on the floor.

Gordon took home the coveted DPOG chain, and with good reason. He's been sensational in these playoffs. He's looking elite in his role as Denver sits just ten wins away from their goal. It's an under-appreciated story outside of our city.

Gordon is a unique player. Few have possessed the tools he does athletically, but his game also has a cerebral element. That aspect of his development went under-nurtured in Orlando, where he was miscast. A player in danger of going down in history as a dunk contest guy teamed up with one of the most brilliant players of all-time. The results are extraordinary. Gordon is becoming his best self and laying the blueprint for anyone wanting to play in Denver. Just listen to Jokic.

Western Conference Semifinals, Game 3

MAY 5, 2023
PHOENIX, ARIZONA
SUNS 121, NUGGETS 114

GLANCING BLOW

WE'RE ABOUT TO FIND OUT WHAT THESE NUGGETS ARE REALLY MADE OF

BY **HARRISON WIND**

Michael Malone can predict the future. At least when it comes to his basketball team.

"We've had no adversity in the postseason, yet," Malone said an hour and a half before Denver and Phoenix tipped off Friday night in Game 3 of their first-round series. "Things have gone really, really smooth. And adversity is coming. It's knocking on the door, and we have to be ready for that. Knowing our guys, I know they will be."

Well, playoff adversity finally came for Denver just as Malone predicted it would. But it didn't politely knock on the proverbial door. It barged through without asking for permission. That's what the Suns' 121-114 Game 3 win over the Nuggets felt like. It was a stark and stern reminder from Devin Booker, who went for 47 points on 20-25 shooting in an individual performance that you could only describe as near-perfect, and Kevin Durant on behalf of the team that was the favorite to win the Western Conference heading into the playoffs.

"Our guys understood that this wasn't going to be a sweep," Malone said postgame. "We weren't just going to beat the Phoenix Suns 4-0. There's a reason that everybody's picking this team to come out of the Western Conference."

Now, this series gets good. Up 2-1 with a chance to put the Suns on life support on Sunday in Game 4 and head back to Denver with a 3-1 lead, now we find out what the Nuggets are really made of. Adversity is here, and now we get to see how Denver responds.

They should rise to the occasion if we think we know what this team is made of, because this is a team that always responds in the face of adversity. This is a team that always bounces back. Nikola Jokic and Jamal Murray know how to show up in the playoffs. Whether it was in the 2020 bubble, when the duo led the Nuggets back from a pair of 3-1 series deficits, or in the first round against Minnesota, they always punch back.

"This team always responds," said Malone. "It's just in our nature."

But the Nuggets will have to be better to beat the Suns on Sunday, and that includes Murray.

Murray took the blame for the Nuggets' Game 3 loss. "I put that on me," he said around 40 minutes after the final buzzer sounded Friday. Murray tallied a team-high 32 points in Game 3 on 13-29 shooting but went only 1-6 from 3-point range. He's now 1-15 from 3 in his last two playoff games. In a pressure-packed second half, Murray shot 6-15. In the fourth quarter, he shot just 1-8.

Many of Murray's Game 3 shot attempts were quality looks. But some weren't.

"I'm just taking what the defense gives me, and trying to make a play," Murray said.

This was Malone's response when asked about Murray's night.

"Jamal was really trying to carry the team tonight. He got off to a tremendous start," Malone said. "He's garnering so much attention out there, and I think when we watch the film, he'll be able to see it. He's doing his job. He's got two defenders on him at times, and that's where he's just got to trust his teammates

Nikola Jokic and the Nuggets were knocked down in the Game 3 loss in Phoenix. (AP Images)

and maybe get off that ball. Because I think a huge part of their game plan is to somehow, some way slow down Jamal Murray and force him into tough shots."

These are tough looks, but also ones Murray can make. The Nuggets even crashed the offensive glass and scored on a couple of those possessions. But Denver can get better shots than these against this Suns' defense. That's the tricky balance here. They can spread it around more.

The Nuggets' defense of course is the No. 1 item on Malone's to-do checklist in terms of what his team has to clean up ahead of Sunday's Game 4. Booker did not feel Denver's defense at all on Friday. Murray said the Nuggets were "discombobulated" when it came to defending Booker. Jokic said the Nuggets played in the first quarter like they were asleep and Booker was able to find a rhythm and explode from there.

However, the Nuggets' offense can use some fine-tuning too, and Game 3 felt like a rare instance where Denver's attack was tilted off its axis. It was slanted too much to Murray and not enough to Jokic and the rest of the Nuggets' offensive options.

During a fourth quarter that while watching it live felt like it was dominated by Murray, I thought back to Jokic's comments from the end of the Timberwolves series and the beginning of this one. Jamal "is our best player," Jokic has said twice during these playoffs. Murray played Game 3 like he was trying to fill the shoes of the Nuggets' "best player," even though we know — and I think Jokic knows — that Murray's not.

This is still Jokic's team. He still needs to be the fulcrum of everything the Nuggets do, even though Denver as a team has taken on Murray's personality in these playoffs. The Nuggets fear no one. They're incredibly confident in themselves and what they can do. Like Murray, they're not surprised with how well they've played in the postseason.

But the Nuggets are being tested for the first time in these playoffs. Now's the time for them to remember the team they are at their core. ⊠

MAY 7, 2023
PHOENIX, ARIZONA
SUNS 129, NUGGETS 124

'IT'S ABOUT PRIDE'

JEFF GREEN CHARTS THE NUGGETS' PATH FORWARD AFTER CONSECUTIVE LOSSES

BY **HARRISON WIND**

After the Mat Ishbia flop, after a jaw-dropping, historic, all-time 53-point performance from Nikola Jokic and after the Nuggets walked off the floor at Footprint Center and silently trudged back to the visiting locker room, veteran Jeff Green offered some words of wisdom about how Denver needs to approach a pivotal and potentially series-deciding Game 5 Tuesday at Ball Arena.

"It's about pride. It's about effort," Green said in a near-empty Nuggets locker room that filtered out quickly after a 129-124 loss. "And it's about wanting to take on the challenge."

I don't know if Green was calling anyone out with those comments — his stern tone certainly suggested he was — but the veteran did pinpoint what needs to change in order for the Nuggets to regain momentum in a now-tied 2-2 series.

The Nuggets have got to take some pride in their defense again. They've got to ramp up their overall intensity. The Suns have become way too comfortable in their last two wins as Denver's defense has fallen way off. The Suns worked the Nuggets again for 20 fast break points in Game 4, just like in Game 3 when they scored 23 points in transition.

Not getting back on defense is just unacceptable at this point in the series. Devin Booker has gotten way too many easy points in transition.

Now, Phoenix has its confidence again, and it means Denver has to go back to the drawing board. Right now, it feels like the Suns know what's coming on both ends of the floor, especially in regard to how Denver is guarding them.

Everyone on the Nuggets has to be better. That includes Aaron Gordon, who's done a solid job on Kevin Durant in this series. That includes Kentavious Caldwell-Pope, Bruce Brown and Christian Braun, Denver's defensive trio that's tasked with checking Booker. That also includes Jamal Murray, who ducked out of the arena and declined to speak with reporters after Game 4.

"I feel like they've kind of figured out what we're trying to do," said Michael Porter Jr.

You'd have to think significant tweaks are in order ahead of Game 5, both in terms of game plan and maybe personnel. Prior to Game 3 of Nuggets-Suns, Denver's bench had been the story of its playoff run. Throughout the Nuggets' first seven playoff games (five vs. Minnesota, two vs. Phoenix) Denver outscored its opponent by 34 points in the 82 minutes that Jokic had been off the floor. But since then, that differential has flipped. The Nuggets are a -19 in the 15 minutes that Jokic has been on the bench over their last two games. Those splits have reverted back to regular-season form.

Can Michael Malone continue to trust his same bench? I don't see how he could with the momentum

Jamal Murray had 28 points, five rebounds and seven assists, but it wasn't enough as the Nuggets dropped Game 4 and saw the series evened up at 2-2. [AP Images]

the Suns have now grabbed and how fatal those minutes have been to the Nuggets over their last two losses.

"We've got to back and look at what we're doing and who we're doing it with," Malone said after Game 4.

Braun, who for my money is the Nuggets' best matchup on Booker, only logged eight minutes in Game 4. That minute total needs to climb in Game 5. If Denver wants more defensive versatility on its second unit, Zeke Nnaji, Vlatko Cancar, or rookie Peyton Watson would be Malone's other possible go-to options if he's thinking about a rotation change (inserting Nnaji and Watson would be my personal choice.) I don't think Malone can risk another debilitating performance from the same bench unit. The Suns have solved that lineup and the Nuggets need to adjust.

The casualty in those scenarios would be Green, who due to Gordon's foul trouble in Game 4 played way too many minutes. Across Games 3 and 4, Denver has been outscored by a staggering 36 points (65-29) in Green's 33 minutes.

It's too bad Denver couldn't bother Booker or Durant much in Game 4. The Nuggets wasted a magical Jokic night where he was the best player in a game that also featured special performances from Booker and Durant. For all the hype about Booker — he's been incredible and deserves the praise he's gotten — Jokic has outscored him 146-145 in the series.

The Nuggets will need more of that Joker magic in Game 5. ⌖

Western Conference Semifinals, Game 5

MAY 9, 2023
DENVER, COLORADO
NUGGETS 118, SUNS 102

TURNING UP THE HEAT

HOW KENTAVIOUS CALDWELL-POPE FINALLY SILENCED DEVIN BOOKER

BY **HARRISON WIND**

It didn't take long to figure out the Nuggets' defensive game plan on Devin Booker in Game 5.

A Booker elbow leading to a Kentavious Caldwell-Pope bloody lip 60 seconds into the first quarter set the tone on Tuesday night.

"I felt like in Games 3 and 4 we weren't physical enough," Caldwell-Pope told *DNVR* after the Nuggets' convincing 118-102 win to take a 3-1 series lead over the Suns. "We weren't into their space or making it tough for them. Tonight, we really just wanted to be more physical. That's how we wanted to play this game."

The scheme Denver deployed on Booker in Game 5 was hatched by Caldwell-Pope, his teammates, and coaching staff in what Michael Malone described as an "interactive" film session after the Nuggets' Game 4 loss. The Nuggets ran through film of Booker dissecting their defense from every angle in Phoenix. Denver's key takeaway from Booker's 36-point performance on 14-18 shooting in Game 4? He got everything too easily. The Nuggets let him get too comfortable. There were just too many instances of Booker walking the ball up the floor, waltzing

into every action, and pummeling Denver's defense without much resistance.

The Nuggets wanted to be more physical in Game 5. They wanted Booker to feel them. They wanted, for once, to tire Booker out and make him work for everything.

"Let's be an irritant," said Michael Malone.

Central to that game plan was Caldwell-Pope, who has taken on the Booker assignment before but wanted the matchup again. Caldwell-Pope knew he could defend Booker better than he has in the series and in Game 5 debuted a new tactic designed to tire him out: A full-court press.

"That was my call," Caldwell-Pope told *DNVR* about picking Booker up full-court for most of Game 5. "I wanted to just lock in defensively because he's averaging almost 40 this series. He's been ridiculous. We know he's going to get his shots. He's going to make tough shots. But for 48 minutes we wanted to keep that pressure on him and keep that physicality."

Even if that physicality meant Caldwell-Pope had to play with a bloody lip for the majority of Game 5.

The results spoke for themselves. Caldwell-

Bruce Brown had a huge game for the Nuggets off the bench in the win with 25 points, five rebounds and four assists.

Aaron Gordon slams home two of his 10 points in the win. While Gordon scored modestly, he was a team-best plus-27 in his 36 minutes on the court.

Pope, who was awarded the Nuggets' Defensive Player of the Game Chain for his defense in Game 5, helped hold Booker to 28 points on 8-19 (42.1%) shooting. It was the first time in 10 playoff games that Booker shot below 47%. Booker eventually tired. Finally. Caldwell-Pope was able to wear him out by sporadically picking him up 94 feet.

"We wanted to make it tough on him the whole game," Caldwell-Pope told *DNVR*. "We don't him to see easy shots or layups go in. When he gets into the lane, foul him hard a couple of times, and let him know that we're still here. It's not going to be easy. He's a tough cover. The more physical we can be, the more we can wear him down throughout the game. That's good for us."

The Nuggets' defense set the tone in Game 5, then Nikola Jokic finished the job. After scoring 10 points on 4-11 shooting in the first half, Jokic tallied 17 of Denver's 39 third-quarter points on 7-8 shooting in a momentum-turning 12 minutes. He finished with 29 points, 13 rebounds and 12 assists, and passed Wilt Chamberlain for most playoff triple-doubles for a center. Jokic has four triple-doubles in these playoffs. No one else in the postseason has more than one.

"He must be stat padding," Malone joked.

After holding the Suns to 102 points on 43.2% shooting, the Nuggets moved to within one victory of their second Western Conference Finals berth in four years.

There's no sugarcoating what was at stake Tuesday at Ball Arena. With the series tied at 2-2, this was the most important game of the Jokic era. Full stop. A win and Denver has the inside track on another Conference Finals appearance where their likely opponent is the seventh-seeded Lakers. A loss and the Nuggets are one defeat away from what would be looked at as a disappointing season. With what's going on in the East — the 76ers and an injured Joel Embiid have the Celtics on the brink of elimination — the Suns right now look like the toughest team Denver will face in these playoffs.

The Nuggets and Malone came through when it mattered.

After all the chatter over the last 48 hours regarding potential changes to the Nuggets' bench rotation, Malone stuck with his same three go-to reserves: Bruce Brown, Christian Braun and Jeff Green. And the second unit was fine. The Nuggets were only outscored by two points with Jokic on the bench in Game 5. But let's not act like Denver's coach sat on his hands and rolled out the same game plan from Game 4. He made adjustments, contrary to what the Twitter coaches will tell you.

The Nuggets mixed up their coverages more on Booker and Kevin Durant. The double teams that Denver sent both Booker and Durant's way were more unpredictable than in Games 3 and 4. Aaron Gordon and Michael Porter Jr. had successful defensive stretches while guarding the Suns' scorers too. The

Nuggets' team defense also leveled up from where it was in Phoenix.

Caldwell-Pope's physicality in the opening minute of Tuesday's win sent a message to Booker that Game 5 was going to be different. The Nuggets hope the rest of the series follows suit.

"I love playing in these types of 1-on-1 matchups," Caldwell-Pope told *DNVR* regarding the Booker assignment. "It's fun. It's like, 'Let's have fun.' Your skills against my skills. I enjoy it. It's just good competition. I love it."

STAR SPOTLIGHT BY BRENDAN VOGT

KENTAVIOUS CALDWELL-POPE – B+

Devin Booker shot just 8-of-19 from the floor. If that appears a minor miracle to you, fair enough. It wasn't an accident, though. More went into that than the law of averages or divine intervention. KCP set the tone early, picking Booker up immediately after the Suns secured the opening tip. Pope forced a loose ball and drew an unpenalized elbow from Booker. The bow drew blood, but Pope was the one sending the message. He spent much of the night hounding Booker up the court. Denver flipped the

Suns' plan of attack on its head. Booker had to work harder on both ends of the floor, and Denver finally held him in check.

Pope's signature hustle reared its head in other ways as well. He got in on the rebounding effort, pulling down seven boards in 27 minutes played. He also drew an offensive foul on a screen, the typical indicator that he's wreaking havoc in Ball Arena. Pope took home the coveted DPOG chain for his excellent night's work.

Western Conference Semifinals, Game 6

MAY 11, 2023
PHOENIX, ARIZONA
NUGGETS 125, SUNS 100

HALFWAY THERE

NUGGETS CRUSH THE SUNS AND CRUISE TO THE WESTERN CONFERENCE FINALS

BY **MIKE OLSON**

**"Believe you can, and you're halfway there."
— Theodore Roosevelt**

If the former Bull Moose Party leader knows anything about anything, these Denver Nuggets and their fanbase must have a lot of belief, because for better and for worse, the team is halfway there.

At the close of last season, and with the looming returns of Jamal Murray and Michael Porter, Jr. on the horizon, team President Josh Kroenke made it known before the offseason truly started that this year had a single goal that would make it a success: the organization's first championship.

Whether that statement was the first domino in the chain of this season, or simply a bellwether of the arc they already knew they were on, the tone was set for this year at every level of the organization.

Coach Michael Malone further stretched his growth curve as a leader, expanding his thinking around past inflexibilities like rookie play, platoon replacements, and more to improve on his abilities and give himself a bevy of options that dismantled his first two series opponents. While there have been numerous players stepping up in waves around superstar Nikola Jokic, Coach Mike and his crew have straight up coached their asses off in the first two rounds and have left the very talented Chris Finch and Monty Williams very much in the dust.

GM Calvin Booth had a vision that surrounded Joker with defenders who could turn around and have a boat-raiser like Jokic raise all of their collective shooting averages in return. What that prescient thought has returned is a team that got a full season to learn exactly how to pull their "string" on defense, transitioning from a bottom-10 defensive squad at season's beginning to a top-10 version after the All-Star Break, up until they did some coasting into the playoffs. Now that every game counts, Denver seems to have answers on the defensive side of the ball that give their opponents difficulties no matter what they attempt.

Two-time (and we biased folks think maybe shoulda been three-time) MVP Nikola Jokic took a set of capabilities that had just earned him All-Galaxy recognition, and somehow bumped it up a notch while Porter and Murray worked their way back into the fold. Ruminate on how complex a task that is, and marvel that Nikola somehow yet again made it look effortless. After an MVP-worthy regular season campaign, his two highest scoring games of these playoffs have been two of Denver's three losses, and he is still somehow wildly outperforming every other player on the stage at this stage. He leads the league in the postseason in category after category, a humble little star from a humble little town outshining all those first-round diamonds. Finding a Jokic in the second round is the equivalent of stumbling upon the Hope Diamond while digging out the space for your septic tank. Who knew you'd find a giant gem amongst the crap you thought you might be sifting through?

Jamal Murray lifted himself back from the doubt of a difficult injury return to the pivotal sand burr of a point guard he'd shown himself to be pre-injury.

Aaron Gordon and the Nuggets blew the Suns off the floor in Game 6, taking the home crowd out of the game in the first quarter. (AP Images)

After two years of toil and reconstruction, Jamal built his game and his bravado back brick by brick, playing through some of the bumps and bruises a younger Malone might have struggled to watch in a regular season campaign. The love and latitude Malone showed his fiery on-court avatar is now paying off in spades, with Murray buoying Denver on a few occasions with his incendiary scoring.

Aaron Gordon took a look the mirror after a season-plus with Jokic and was man enough to realize he still had some basketball IQ to gain. Whatever summer school AG went to deserves a 50 in its own right, as AG has been a man possessed on the defensive side of the ball all season and all playoffs long and contributing on the offensive end as a former-first-and-now-often-fifth option. When Murray and MPJ were finding their sea legs, and Kentavious Caldwell-Pope and Bruce Brown were still learning what Jokic-Ball made truly possible, Gordon was the

second fiddle and stalwart through the first third of this Nuggets season, carrying them until they started getting the larger offensive engine to truly fire. The flexibility and humility of Mr. Nugget is an oft-underrated key to this season's overall success.

Michael Porter, Jr heard the criticisms and attentions to his past game, and spent his recovery time in Study Hall, learning more of the defensive game while he was down so he could become a more complete player as he worked his way back into game shape. Porter was also the beneficiary of a longer leash from Malone, which has paid off in the most complete basketball of his career. Mike is no longer a defensive liability, with length, intelligence, and speed to spare. Mike is now more often a plus on both ends of the floor. Shooting slumps no longer portend a vanishing act, which is also why Porter is rarely a minus on the stat sheet any longer. With those additions, he has become the perfect relief valve to the Murray/Jokic two man game and should only be a larger part of that whirlygig as the trio moves forward.

Kentavious Caldwell-Pope has a ring and wants another and has been preaching the path to his teammates all season. He might have displayed more heart, grit, and fire than anyone in the last two games that closed out the Phoenix series. Devin Booker might have certainly said so if he'd decided to chat with anyone in the media before ducking out of the building after the Suns' season set.

Bruce Brown drank the Kool-Aid that Booth and Malone were selling in the offseason and came into a situation ready-made for his skills. Brown also sacrificed a ton this season to be a part of a bigger picture, and is exactly the type of get-it-done role player the team had envisioned in pulling him in.

Even a rookie like Christian Braun has played the game inside the lines Malone has delineated for him after a season's seasoning and flourished. Jeff Green levitated at least once a night to entertain the crowds, but more importantly stay in the younger guys ears. Role players, veterans, and vocal leaders like DeAndre Jordan, Vlatko Čančar, Reggie Jackson and Ish Smith

have stayed vocal and supportive of their teammates while they have navigated the ups and downs of a 53-win season now combined with their first eight wins of these playoffs. Everyone has played their part.

It does feel different this year, doesn't it? Even if they don't somehow win it all, this one feels different. Like these are just the first eight wins of this journey. A repeating journey, by the way, that these Nuggets have never managed more than 10 wins in since they joined the NBA. Do they have eight more in them? It feels more possible than it ever has.

They sure look like a team that is unimpressed by what they've accomplished so far, even after a 25-point drubbing of a team that embarrassed you a couple years prior. I love it. It's not that this victory isn't worth celebrating, and I'm sure the team will. For the first time, it doesn't feel like maybe this is all the Denver Nuggets can do. Whether they complete the task this year or not, for the first time, it feels like maybe this is just halfway. ⊠

STAR SPOTLIGHT BY BRENDAN VOGT
NIKOLA JOKIC – A+

How will the Denver Nuggets guard the Phoenix Suns? That question was often asked after the Suns pulled the trigger on a blockbuster deal to acquire Kevin Durant. They'll run a thousand pick-and-rolls. They'll target Nikola Jokic and Michael Porter Jr. relentlessly. They'll expose Denver's precarious defense. Phoenix had the shiny exterior of a new contender and quickly leapfrogged a bonafide one in Denver. Remember, the Suns were favored heading into the series.

Of course, the pundits were asking the wrong question the entire time. How were the Suns to guard the best player in the world? They never had an answer. While Devin Booker touched God in the middle of the series, Jokic set up camp in the

realm of the divine. He lived there, withstanding the onslaught and standing tall as the best player in the series when the dust settled. He was nearly flawless offensively. He played a tremendous series defensively. He did it all while emanating an eerie calmness. Jokic was in control from the opening tip.

It's onto the next mountain for the giant from Sombor. The Ayton narrative is old news. His defense looks better than ever. He's got as much left in the tank as we've seen from him this late in the season. We're watching the best player on the planet hit a level few have ever reached. Our wildest dreams and predictions for his career pale in comparison to reality. Try your best not to take it for granted. We may never see this again.

Western Conference Finals, Game 1

MAY 16, 2023
DENVER, COLORADO
NUGGETS 132, LAKERS 126

'I JUST WANT TO WIN'

MICHAEL PORTER JR.'S WILLING TO DO WHATEVER IT TAKES

BY **HARRISON WIND**

Michael Malone called it one of the most consequential plays of Game 1. Nikola Jokic called it simply "playoff basketball."

Michael Porter Jr.'s pivotal 50-50 loose ball recovery late in the fourth quarter was one of the defining moments from the Nuggets' 132-126 win over the Lakers. Without it, the Nuggets might be trailing 0-1 in the series right now.

"I just remember getting on the floor for it. It easily could have been a jump ball," Porter said. "I just tried my hardest to get the ball to my teammates through the crowd."

He succeeded. Porter was able to shovel the ball off to Kentavious Caldwell-Pope, who fired it ahead to Jamal Murray, whose pinpoint alley-oop lob from outside the 3-point line feet greeted Aaron Gordon at the rim. Ball Arena erupted.

"It was big. It was very big," said Murray. "It was a momentum swinger."

But it all started with Porter's hustle. If he doesn't come up with that loose ball, the Nuggets may have choked away the 20+ point lead that they played with for most of Game 1. It would have been an epic and maybe fatal collapse, one that I'm not sure the Nuggets ultimately recover from.

That wasn't the only extra-effort play that Porter made. Playing through knee soreness and what Porter described postgame as "some other things going on,"

the forward got on the glass for 10 rebounds (three offensive) and used his length to send back two Laker shot attempts. He also tallied 15 points and was one of six Nuggets players in double-figure scoring.

Porter's two blocks were textbook. He used his length perfectly.

Porter's game was symbolic of the Nuggets' current team-wide mentality as Denver took a 1-0 lead over Los Angeles in the Western Conference Finals. The Nuggets are showing that they're willing to put it all on the line for a victory. It's that time of year. Egos are pushed aside. Point totals don't matter. Individual statistics aren't on anyone's mind. The entire locker room is bought in.

Its why Porter went to Malone during Round 2 of the playoffs vs. the Suns and said he was fine if Malone opted to close fourth quarters with Bruce Brown in his place. "I just want to win," Porter told Denver's coach. Of course, Porter wants to be on the floor, but he's fine relinquishing his spot to Brown if that's what Malone thinks gives the Nuggets the best chance at a victory.

"It's just about winning," Porter said Tuesday.

With Porter setting the tone with his hustle and selfless attitude, the Nuggets are in great shape. Murray's already playing through an illness and painful ear infection, which he's had since Saturday. He still found a way to go for 31 points. Battling

Michael Porter Jr. had 15 points and 10 rebounds in the Game 1 win, but also did the little things unseen in the box score to contribute to the victory.

through various bumps and bruises of his own, Jokic did what he usually does in the playoffs — post a historic stat line in a win.

The sickness that Murray's dealing with has been making its way through the Nuggets locker room — Malone's voice has been hoarse for over a week — and got to Porter in Phoenix. He felt under the weather in Games 3 and 4 vs. the Suns.

"At this point," said Porter. "Our mentality is to battle through anything."

The Nuggets are pushing through it all. And in the process, Porter's taking on some traits of his two-time MVP running mate, who's never had an excuse for anything, both on and off the court. How Porter played Game 1 vs. the Lakers was so unlike the player that he was when he entered the NBA. He played physical, tough, and composed basketball. He wasn't rattled. Porter was ready for the moment, just as his entire

team has been throughout the playoffs. He was willing to do whatever it takes to win, just as Jokic is every single night.

And that brings me to the final note on Porter's evening. He arrived and departed Ball Arena Tuesday in a suit, like Jokic typically does every game — Porter wore a sleek black coat and pants and paired them with jet-black Prada shoes.

As Porter left the locker room after Game 1, Jokic chuckled. It's not an outfit that he apparently would try to pull off, but Jokic did appreciate Porter opting for formal wear.

He approved.

"It was good. It was good," Jokic said about Porter's suit. "He's picking it up." 🖼

Western Conference Finals, Game 2

MAY 18, 2023
DENVER, COLORADO
NUGGETS 108, LAKERS 103

TAKING THEIR RESPECT

JAMAL MURRAY AND THE NUGGETS WANT YOU TO KNOW THEY'RE READY FOR THIS

BY **HARRISON WIND**

Jamal Murray tried to warn you. He told everyone who was willing to listen. He broadcasted it to the entire world.

"We're ready for this!" Murray yelled to the Ball Arena crowd after his dagger 3 sealed the Nuggets' Game 1 win over the Suns three weeks ago.

Everyone thought the Nuggets weren't ready for this spotlight, these expectations and these types of playoff-tested, star-studded, championship-contending playoff opponents. Some even picked Denver to lose in the first round to Minnesota. The Nuggets entered the second round vs. the Suns as underdogs. After their Game 1 win over the Lakers, the national narrative circled back to LeBron James, Anthony Davis and how Rui Hachimura's six fourth-quarter possessions of defense against Nikola Jokic meant Denver was in trouble.

The Nuggets took note, then came out and won a hard-fought Game 2.

"I think a lot of our guys, to be honest, they may not admit this or not. You win Game 1, and all everybody talked about was the Lakers," Michael Malone said after the Nuggets' 108-103 win Thursday night. "Let's be honest, the national narrative was 'Hey, the Lakers are fine. They're down 1-0, but they figured something out.'"

The Nuggets are walking, talking, and playing with a type of confidence that I've never seen from

them before. They're cocky. They're bold. They're fearless. After Game 1, Bruce Brown called out D'Angelo Russell's defense after the Nuggets played him off the floor in the fourth quarter. Michael Porter Jr. casually dismissed the successful adjustment that the Lakers made. Prior to Game 2, Malone lambasted the Hachimura storyline.

"Even when we win," Murray said. "They talk about the other team."

Who are these guys?

Here's my read: This is a group that's been waiting for this moment. The Nuggets have heard everything that's been said about them over the last three seasons — from the pundits who discredited Jokic's back-to-back MVPs and claimed he'd get exposed on defense in the playoffs, to the lack of respect for the Nuggets as true contenders this season — and now they're acting on it.

Murray has been ticked off all year about the constant comparisons to "Bubble Murray" and the questions about whether or not he's fully "back." Denver's locker room has felt disrespected by the lack of attention they've received as the No. 1 seed in the West, a spot they've held since December.

The Nuggets have said that they'll show the world who they really are in the playoffs, Now, it's all coming out. And as Murray proclaimed, they're ready for this.

"We play like the No. 1 seed and we believe we're

the No. 1 seed," said Murray. "And we back it up."

The Nuggets' Game 2 win was a championship-level victory from a group that looks more and more like a team of destiny. Nothing went right for Denver in the first half of Game 2. The Nuggets were in foul trouble, Denver couldn't hit from 3, and no one outside of Jokic, who recorded his fourth-straight triple-double in Game 2 and seventh of the playoffs, could find an offensive rhythm. Then, Murray hit a pull-up jumper with 10 minutes left in the fourth quarter with the Nuggets trailing 81-79 and everything changed.

Murray scored 23 of his 37 points in the fourth. He drained eight of his final nine shots of Game 2. He erupted. His fourth-quarter flurry led to what I think is the loudest I've ever heard Ball Arena. It was Murray's fourth career 20+ point fourth quarter in the playoffs, the most of any player over the last 25 years.

"To have a closer like Jamal is definitely something that we cherish," Malone said.

This is the team that Malone, Jokic and Murray have been waiting three years for. It's the team that this organization and city have envisioned all along. This is what the Nuggets were meant to be. On Thursday, Denver moved two wins away from its first Finals appearance in franchise history and six wins away from its first NBA championship. Injuries stalled the Nuggets' timeline, but now Denver is back on track.

"It delayed our destiny and our journey," said Malone.

Following the Nuggets' 97-87 Game 2 win vs. the Suns — a win that felt eerily similar to Thursday's Game 2 triumph over the Lakers — I spoke with a member of the Nuggets' front office who has been with this team for the majority of the Jokic era.

"After Game 1, I thought we could definitely win the series," he told *DNVR*. "After Game 2, I thought we could definitely win the championship."

This Game 2 win over the Lakers gave off that same feeling.

The Nuggets still have several more steps to climb. The job is not close to complete. Game 3 Saturday in Los Angeles is going to be the most difficult game the Nuggets have played all postseason and Denver is going to have to play its best game of the playoffs to win.

But this team believes, and they think you're a fool if you don't. So either get on board or get left behind.

"Same old, same old. It just fuels us a little more," Murray said regarding the narrative that emerged after Game 1. "And it will be sweeter when we win the 'Chip." 🖼

MAY 20, 2023
LOS ANGELES, CALIFORNIA
NUGGETS 119, LAKERS 108

NEVER A DOUBT

NIKOLA JOKIC AND THE NUGGETS ARE DOING IT THEIR WAY

BY **HARRISON WIND**

To beat the Lakers in Game 3 of the Western Conference Finals and to come within one win of their first-ever NBA Finals, the Nuggets could only do it one way: Their way.

Jamal Murray's 30 first-half points set Denver up, but the Nuggets were never going to finish the job like that. Because at their core, that's not who these Denver Nuggets are. They're at their best when they're operating as one. They're a team in every sense of the word. And that's why the Nuggets captured their biggest win in franchise history Saturday night.

This was the most pivotal sequence of Game 3, to me at least. With the Nuggets barely holding onto a two-point lead and seven minutes remaining in regulation, Denver's selfless, team basketball was put on display.

Michael Porter Jr. passed up a long two-point jump shot that he drains in his sleep and made an extra pass to Bruce Brown in the corner. Brown promptly drained the 3, silencing the Lakers' crowd (again). It was an early dagger. The Nuggets never looked back. Michael Malone called it one of his "favorite" plays of the night. It was the ultimate look that went from good to great with an extra pass.

In total, the Nuggets tallied 30 assists in Game 3, their third-most of the playoffs. None might have been more important than that one.

"I love it, just because you can see everybody's moving," Nikola Jokic said of Denver's passing. "I think that's hard to guard."

"It's so, how do you say it, when you, like poison?" continued Jokic looking for just the right word. "It's contagious. Yeah, and I love it. I think that's the best brand of basketball. At least everybody enjoying."

If the Nuggets were going to pull off the improbable feat of winning an NBA championship, they were always going to do it this way. With everyone pulling in one direction. With chemistry, culture and a team-first mindset. They were never going to be the 2013 Miami Heat with LeBron James. They were always going to be the 2014 San Antonio Spurs, the team that ended the Heat's reign in five games in the Finals that year.

Murray carried Denver in the first half, then the Nuggets took over. Jokic scored 19 points in the second half and 15 in the fourth quarter. Brown had 15. Kentavious Caldwell-Pope put in 17. Jeff Green tallied five points, four rebounds, closed the fourth quarter over Aaron Gordon and converted a massive 3-pointer in the fourth right before Brown's game-turning shot.

"We're just a very unselfish team," Murray said. "It may not be your night, it may not be your quarter."

Game 3 was a Nuggets win for the ages. It felt

Michael Malone's Nuggets took control of the series in Game 3, winning comfortably in Los Angeles, 119-108. [AP Images]

like everything was against them. The narrative, the officiating, and Denver even survived a subpar Jokic first half. But the Nuggets found a way. That's what this team does.

"I learn a lot about this team every time we play," Caldwell-Pope said.

They never got rattled and they never lost faith. Denver was as resilient as ever.

"I never doubt my team," said Jokic.

The Nuggets have the look of a team of destiny. It feels like nothing can stop them, and they know it too. They sense it. They believe. All playoffs, the Nuggets have exuded an incredible amount of confidence. They know what they have, and now the rest of the country does too.

"It takes 16 wins to win a championship," Murray said. "We've got five more to go, and the Lakers are in our way. And they're going to do everything in their power to come back and fight."

"We've got five more to go." 🖼

MAY 22, 2023
LOS ANGELES, CALIFORNIA
NUGGETS 113, LAKERS 111

'HE'S A BASKETBALL GOD'

INSIDE NIKOLA JOKIC'S GAME 4 MASTERPIECE

BY **HARRISON WIND**

What's there left to say about Nikola Jokic at this point?

After a 30-point, 14-rebound, 13-assist triple-double on a night where he broke Wilt Chamberlain's 56-year-old record for most triple-doubles in a single playoffs and willed the Nuggets to a four-game sweep over the Lakers, there's simply nothing else.

Incredible. Inconceivable. Impossible. Once in a lifetime. Jokic does not seem real at this point. But how does one of the few people who's been by the two-time MVP's side throughout his entire eight-year career describe the greatest player on the planet and what he's been able to do this postseason?

"He's a basketball God," Nuggets assistant coach Ogi Stojakovic told *DNVR* on the way out of Crypto. com Arena late Monday night.

Stojakovic is one of the few members of the Nuggets' organization who was in Denver when Jokic arrived in the Mile High City in 2015. He was originally hired by former GM Tim Connelly prior to the Nuggets even drafting Jokic because Connelly thought there could be an influx of European players entering Denver's pipeline. But once Jokic came to Denver, Stojakovic, who is also from Serbia, became a key figure in his development.

"He never stops amazing me," Stojakovic told *DNVR*. "He never stops."

Watching Jokic in the Western Conference Finals was a spiritual experience. He averaged 27.8 points (50.6 FG%, 47.1 3P%), 14.5 rebounds, 11.8 assists per game, 1.8 blocks, and 1.8 steals per game. He transformed into a higher being. His stats don't seem from this world.

In the playoffs, he's averaging the 5th-most points, the 2nd-most rebound, and leads the postseason in assists and +/- despite averaging the 12th-most minutes per game. In four games against the Lakers, Jokic scored or assisted on 88 of the 156 (that's 56.4%) baskets that the Nuggets scored when he was on the floor. After Jokic dropped 34 points on 12-17 shooting in Game 1, the Lakers were forced to switch "All-World" defender Anthony Davis off of him. That battleground was decided after 48 minutes.

How Jokic conducted this series was beautiful. He's the only player in the NBA right now who manipulates almost every possession that his team plays. No one else has this kind of influence over their group. No one else's fingerprints are all over everything that their team does like Jokic's are. It's something that we haven't seen in this league in a long, long time.

BASKETBALL GOD
MVP
MVP
X2
2000
POINTS
1000
REBOUNDS
500
ASSISTS
BIGHONEY

"He's a maestro with the basketball," Aaron Gordon said of Jokic. "He's a savant."

On defense, he more than held his own. We're awaiting Game 1 of the Finals, and Jokic still hasn't been played off the floor defensively. Opposing offenses still haven't been able to put him in a million pick-and-roll and expose the Nuggets on that end of the floor. One of the most laughable storylines around Jokic entering the playoffs has officially been proven false and can be put to rest for good. Jokic is a fine playoff defender, which is something that those who actually watch him already knew.

"I think it's self-explanatory, brother," said Jamal Murray when asked about what Jokic has done this postseason.

In the series, Jokic held Anthony Davis to 49.1% shooting when he was Davis' primary defender. By the end of Game 4 — a game where Davis shot 6-15 while not even guarding Jokic on the other end of the floor — it looked like Davis wanted to throw in the towel. He had had enough. Jokic will wear you out mentally and physically during a playoff series. That's what he did to Davis.

"He's developed into an all-timer in a rapid amount of time," Nuggets general manager Calvin Booth told *DNVR* after Game 4. "When I got here, there were a lot of big guys over him. And now there's not."

No one can do what Jokic does, and he's the only one who hits these types of shots with regularity.

Remember his third-quarter stunner in Game 1?

Then in Game 4 with less than three minutes on the clock, he nailed the shot of the playoffs.

Those were Basketball God-like.

The narrative around Jokic has shifted. He's proving all of his doubters wrong and all of his believers right. Jokic has now taken down Donovan

LeBron James and the Lakers tried to make it hard on Nikola Jokic all series but to no avail as the Nuggets competed the sweep on the Lakers' home court. (AP Images)

Mitchell, Rudy Gobert (twice), Kawhi Leonard, Paul George, Damian Lillard, CJ McCollum, Karl-Anthony Towns, Anthony Edwards, Kevin Durant, Devin Booker, Chris Paul, and now LeBron James and Anthony Davis in the playoffs. During his first-ever playoff run, Jokic beat a veteran Spurs team coached by Gregg Popovich and led by LaMarcus Aldridge and DeMar DeRozan. It's a hell of a resume, and Jokic is just 28 years old.

"I think he's showing other people nationally that he's real. Like what he's doing is real," Michael Malone said. "The MVPs are real. The triple-doubles are real. The narratives, the silly narratives this year are just what, silly and somewhat ignorant. He's a great player, and give him the respect he deserves."

How Jokic has carried himself in these playoffs — amid those narratives and with an enormous amount of pressure on his shoulders — has been stunning. He has been unbothered. He almost laughs it off. And what pressure? Of course, Jokic doesn't feel it. He doesn't feel the weight of the world on his shoulders. Jokic always says that he never stresses or gets nervous about taking game-winning shots with no time on the clock simply because his only option in those situations is to shoot the ball. He just goes out there and performs. He's just focused on doing what it takes to win.

There's still more of this journey to go. Of course, Jokic celebrated after sweeping the Lakers, first with his brothers and family in the stands, and then on the court with his teammates and coaches. Then, he hit the weight room in the bowels of the Lakers' arena.

Because while getting to the Finals was a goal of his, there's still one more box this season to check. The job isn't quite finished. ⌂

Nikola Jokic holds the Magic Johnson Trophy for the MVP of the Western Conference Finals as his teammates celebrate his dominant series. (AP Images)

All the Nuggets Are Good.